WHAT WOULD

JESUS

Drink?

Brad Whittington

What they're saying about
What Would Jesus Drink?

The expert of all experts, Brad Whittington, conservative Christian oenophile has made an astoundingly exhaustive study of every alcohol reference in Scripture.
—A.J. Jacobs, AJJacobs.com, author of *The Know-It-All, The Year of Living Biblically,* and *My Life as an Experiment*

I can't give Brad enough credit for all his hard work on finding the truth within this touchy subject matter. His research has been painstaking, and I'd encourage everyone to explore his work.
—J. Wilson, Brewvana.WordPress.com, author of *Diary of a Part-Time Monk*

This comprehensive survey of the biblical teaching on alcohol use is a must-have resource. Top notch. Distribute widely please.
—Michael Spencer, InternetMonk.com, author of *Mere Churchianity: Finding Your Way Back to Jesus-Shaped Spirituality*

Thorough, balanced, and fair, this small book will serve as a reference for Christians who want to know exactly what the Bible says about wine and strong drink. By organizing and analyzing every scriptural mention of the topic, Brad Whittington equips and encourages believers to go beyond contemporary cultural influences to draw biblically based conclusions. Highly recommended.
—Kathy Tyers, author of *The Annotated Firebird, Shivering World*, and other novels

It's amazing to me how often Christians form their convictions about alcohol based on culture, family history, or in reaction to someone else's position. Brad Whittington gets his conviction from somewhere else: a staggeringly thorough study of every verse in the Bible that mentions alcohol. His book is a must-read for teetotalers and frat boys alike.
—Noel Heikkinen, JustNoel.com, pastor, Riverview Church

Very enlightening research with timely and balanced information concerning the way in which a Christian should handle the issue of alcohol use. On-target concerning this issue.
—Matt Layton, OnceInAGreatWhile.BlogSpot.com

This is an article that you and all of your Christian friends should read.
—Theological Persiflage, PersiflageThis.BlogSpot.com

Also by Brad Whittington

Welcome To Fred

Living with Fred

Escape From Fred

CONTENTS

For Daniel:

Who plied the needful to the not-so-bitter end

Therefore do not let anyone judge you by what you eat or drink, or with regard to a religious festival, a New Moon celebration, or a Sabbath day. Colossians 2:16

The one who eats everything must not treat with contempt the one who does not, and the one who does not eat everything must not judge the one who does, for God has accepted them. Who are you to judge someone else's servant? To their own master, servants stand or fall. And they will stand, for the Lord is able to make them stand. Romans 14:3-4

INTRODUCTION *What would Jesus drink?*

In 1996, in the height of the What Would Jesus Do? movement, I found myself wondering about the answer to this question in relation to drinking wine, beer, and liquor.

I was raised Southern Baptist, the son of a seminary-educated preacher who was one of maybe a half dozen people in the country who could read ancient Sumerian cuneiform. It was not a skill in great demand in the Big Thicket of East Texas, and being the son of a man with this distinction didn't gather me any respect among my classmates in Fred, Texas, where I grew up in the 1970s.

Texas has this thing called the local option election, whereby each county decides locally whether to allow the sale of alcohol. As a teenager, I participated in successful campaigns to keep our county dry, another accomplishment that failed to garner respect from my peers. I was probably the only kid in my graduating class who had never tasted alcohol. Or smoked. Or danced. These kinds of things were an occupational hazard for a Southern Baptist preacher's kid.

But the question of what Jesus would drink is not the exclusive domain of Southern Baptist PKs. A surprising number of people have found themselves in an argument on this question.

Was Jesus really the miraculous bartender, as some have said, by creating wine at a wedding? Did Jesus really drink wine at the Last Supper? Was the wine in the Bible really grape juice? Is drinking wine, beer, or liquor a sin, or is it just a personal preference? Should a Christian abstain anyway, even if it's not a sin?

This topic has been ruffling feathers for over a century in the United States and perhaps even longer. Back in 1874, women concerned about the destructive power of alcohol and the problems it caused their families and society founded the Woman's Christian Temperance Union (WCTU) in Cleveland, Ohio. WCTU members chose total abstinence from alcohol as their lifestyle and adopted the Greek philosopher Xenophon's definition of temperance:

> Temperance may be defined as: moderation in all things healthful; total abstinence from all things harmful. - Xenophon, c. 400 BCE

What would Jesus drink? Regardless of the answer, there is no question about the significant and frequently negative effect of alcohol on families and society.

Sobering Statistics

This section gives some statistics on the damaging effects of alcohol on society as of this writing. If you're not into statistics, skip to Mixed Messages.

You don't have to try very hard to find all kinds of negative statistics associated with alcohol. Almost everyone has had a friend or family member die due to drunk driving. The US Department of Transportation reports that in 2009, one-third of traffic fatalities (10,839 out of 33,808) were due to drunken driving, 1,077 of those being teenagers.

According to the 2007 report Deaths: Final Data for 2007 from the Centers for Disease Control and Prevention (CDC):

- 14,406 people died from alcoholic liver disease
- 23,199 people died from alcohol-induced deaths, excluding accidents and homicides

Consider these statistics from About-Alcohol-Abuse.com:

Crimes/Injuries/Deaths

- In 2001, more than half a million people were injured in crashes where police reported that alcohol was present.
- The National Highway Traffic Safety Administration estimates that there were 17,000 alcohol-related traffic fatalities in each of the last three years.
- Fifty percent of US homicides are alcohol related.
- Forty percent of US assaults are alcohol related.
- More than 100,000 US deaths are caused by excessive alcohol consumption each year through drunk driving, cirrhosis of the liver, falls, cancer, stroke, and others.

Costs

- Alcoholism causes 500 million lost workdays a year.
- Alcohol dependence and alcohol abuse cost the US an estimated $220 billion in 2005. This dollar amount was more than the cost associated with obesity ($133 billion) or with cancer ($196 billion).
- Underage drinking costs Americans nearly $53 billion annually.

No matter what comes of this inquiry, no one can deny that these numbers are horrifying. If we were attempting to discover whether alcohol has caused a lot of damage, heartache, illness, and death, we could stop right now. The answer is quite clearly yes.

But this is a search for what the Bible says about drinking, so we must look to the Scriptures, not statistics.

Mixed Messages

What would Jesus drink? As every new generation arrives at the age of majority, the question is asked again. For the sincere follower of Jesus, the answer is not as easy to find as one might expect.

As with other doctrines, the stance of the church on this topic varies by denomination. While all denominations caution against drunkenness, some have no proscription on alcohol consumption while others prohibit the use of alcohol altogether.

If we look to the history of the attitude of the church toward drinking, we find equally confusing positions. The Catholic church has a long history of endorsing a moderate use of alcohol. The founders of the Reformation were enthusiastic drinkers. But there are also major figures in church history who have stood strongly against the consumption of alcohol and used the Scriptures to back their position.

I haven't found an exhaustive history on ecclesiastical attitudes toward alcohol, but I suspect that the current ambivalence on the topic stretches back to the beginnings of Christianity and beyond. We will look more into this topic in the chapter on the conservative Christian subculture.

So we must turn to the Scripture itself to find what it says on this subject. But even a sincere follower of Jesus who wants to learn what the Bible really says and is committed to following the full counsel of Scripture on drinking faces a daunting task. Anybody can find individual verses and try to discern the message, but in my search to answer the question, I found that early on things get tricky.

For example, how is one to interpret these verses?

> May God give you heaven's dew and earth's richness—an abundance of grain and new wine.
> Genesis 27:28

> Should I give up my wine, which cheers both gods and humans? Judges 9:13

> Wine that gladdens human hearts. Psalm 104:15

When compared to these verses?

> Wine is a mocker and beer a brawler; whoever is led astray by them is not wise. Proverbs 20:1

> Do not join those who drink too much wine. Proverbs 23:20

> Do not get drunk on wine, which leads to debauchery. Ephesians 5:18

As you read, it's easy to find warnings against drunkenness, but then you run up against the story in John 2 where Jesus made over a hundred gallons of wine at a wedding where the crowd was already tipsy.

A seeker can't be blamed for being confused. After all, how many people have the time to search through the 800,000+ words in the Bible to discover the big picture, the full message on this topic when taken as a whole?

Digging Deeper

That's where this book comes in. I had the same questions, and I came up against the same problems in finding a definitive answer.

Twenty years after high school, twenty years of regular membership in Southern Baptist churches, I decided to dig deeper, to find every verse in the Bible that touched on this topic, and figure it out. I set aside any sermons I might have heard, any personal history, any personal preference, and began a search for the truth, committed to following it wherever it might lead.

This book is the chronicle of that search and my conclusions. Here you will find all 247 verses of the Bible that reference wine and strong drink listed and categorized. You will also find my analysis and conclusions. However, I'm not saying you should come to the same conclusions. My background notwithstanding, I am not a biblical scholar by any definition of the term. I am merely an ordinary Christian trying to figure this out in a tradition-free, culture-free context.

Think of this book as a starting point for your own research, analysis, and deliberation. You have to make your own decision, guided and informed by the Scripture. Like the Bereans in Acts 17, you should search the Scriptures for yourself to find what is true. This book makes that easier by gathering all the verses together and providing a little organization to streamline your study.

I have also included my impressions and conclusions as I worked my way through the verses. But you should take care to separate The Word from my words, and the source material from my conclusions.

If you read the verses and come to a different conclusion, that's fine. I hope that we can agree to disagree, according each other the respect due to one who seeks after truth in good will and good faith, as Paul says.

> The one who eats everything must not treat with contempt the one who does not, and the one who does not eat everything must not judge the one who does, for God has accepted them. Who are you to judge someone else's servant? To their own master, servants stand or fall. And they will stand, for the Lord is able to make them stand. Romans 14:3-4

CULTURE OR SCRIPTURE? It's impor-

that we begin with a clear understanding of the goal. From the beginning of my research, my goal was to find the truth as defined by Scripture, and that is the target of this short book.

If the current culture in which we live is a deciding factor in your search, you may as well stop reading right now. In fact, if that's the case, send me an e-mail, and I'll refund your money or send you one of my other books free as compensation, because the money you spent on this book will have been wasted.

For my purposes, culture was not relevant to the inquiry, whether the prevailing culture of society or the culture of the church. Especially the culture of the church, because often it is difficult for insiders to differentiate between what the Bible says and what church tradition says, and these two are not necessarily the same thing.

As any thinking person realizes immediately, an institution as old as the church, or even as old as a single denomination, develops a culture. It acquires thoughts and practices, and they become engrained in the corporate culture. These thoughts and practices become almost indistinguishable from, but not equivalent to, the original principles. I wasn't interested in the barnacles encrusted on the ship of faith. I wanted the word pure from the source.

As Paul says, we should not conform to the pattern of the world, but be transformed by the renewing of the mind, rejecting cultural standards in preference of scriptural standards of behavior.

> Do not conform to the pattern of this world, but be transformed by the renewing of your mind. Then you will be able to test and approve what God's will is— his good, pleasing and perfect will. Romans 12:2

Jesus criticized the Pharisees for multiplying rules and requirements for people to follow while setting an even more exacting standard for the believer. Of the legalistic believers of his day, Jesus said:

> They tie up heavy, cumbersome loads and put them on other people's shoulders, but they themselves are not willing to lift a finger to move them. Matthew 23:4

But he took things to the next level, not giving his followers an easy out, when he said:

> Be perfect, therefore, as your heavenly Father is perfect. Matthew 5:48

That sounds like an even heavier requirement, but the point was that true faith is a matter of the heart, not a matter of following rules. It's easy to consult a checklist to see if you're safe. It's quite another matter to daily examine your heart to see if you're following the law of love.

My aim was to strike the path of righteousness based on the law of love while avoiding the ditches on either side, neither imposing cultural mores as scriptural mandates, nor dismissing scriptural principles in favor of cultural preferences.

For example, there is no warning in the Bible against dancing, but some denominations, like my own, teach against dancing. Due to my background, I've never been much of a dancer, but despite some protestations to the contrary, it is clear to me that this is a cultural preference, not a scriptural principle. I would say that opposition to dancing on cultural grounds is not a problem as long as it is not presented as a scriptural principle or biblical imperative.

On the other hand, there are many passages in the Bible that speak against adultery, Exodus 20 being the most popular.

You shall not commit adultery. Exodus 20:14

Many argue that biblical standards of sexual morality are not relevant to modern society. However, there is no expiration date on the Ten Commandments. As one preacher said, the new morality is just the old immorality. The Bible is very clear on the issue of adultery. Christians who are intent on discerning and living the full counsel of Scripture have opposed the reclassification of adultery as a cultural preference.

Reading with an Agenda

There are many reasons people pick up a book like this one. Perhaps you're curious. You've never thought about the issue, and you're interested in finding out what the Bible says. In that case, you're probably in the minority, but you've come to the right place.

Perhaps you're a militant abstainer and you're looking for ammunition in your crusade to convict sinners of their transgressions and guilt them into holiness. In that case, you're out of luck. This book is more about the heart than the rules.

Or you may be looking for a permission slip from Jesus to prove that you have the scriptural right to do what you've already decided you're going to do. You're also out of luck. No free passes here.

You could be struggling with alcohol abuse and looking for excuses to avoid dealing with it by showing that the Bible says it's OK. I hope not, because we both know that's just a delaying tactic and a dangerous way to live. This book doesn't hold the answer to your problem.

Or perhaps you live with someone who has a drinking problem and you're hoping to find something in here that will help you persuade him or her to get help. My heart goes out to you. I wish I had the answer that would fix things for you. There are people qualified to address that issue, but I'm not one of them, and this is not that book.

Or maybe you've heard a lot of preaching about the topic, perhaps even contradictory messages, and you're confused about what the Bible really says. Maybe you want to find out so you can act on it in faith. In that case, this is the book for you.

If you're willing to set aside your preconceptions and take a journey of discovery to find the true intent of the Bible, I think you'll find this little book worthwhile.

Getting Down to It

The question before me when I embarked on this study was the scriptural position on alcohol. And that is what we'll look at now. Not what your daddy or my daddy thought and taught. Not what your denomination or my denomination publishes in their literature. What the Scripture says.

What would Jesus drink? Some Christians consider moderate use of alcohol to be completely acceptable, while others consider any use of alcohol whatsoever to be sinful. Which position is scriptural, and which is cultural? Or perhaps both are cultural and there is a third scriptural position.

In answering this question, our primary focus is the Bible itself. We will look at all the references to wine and strong drink in the Bible, and we will examine the life of Jesus. We will also look at the common arguments that arise in a discussion on this topic. All quotations are from the New International Version (NIV) unless otherwise noted.

ANALYSIS OF SCRIPTURAL Refer-

ences to Alcohol. My first step in the journey was to locate all the relevant verses in the Bible. In the Old and New Testament there are 228 references to wine and 19 references to strong drink. That's a lot of information to synthesize, so I organized them into categories as indicated below. You can find all the verses listed in the appendix.

I spent many hours digging through all these verses, and if you want the full story, you should look at them all too. But don't worry about your eyes glazing over in the next few sections. I worked up a summary of the highlights for quick reading. After the table there is a quick summary of the numbers, followed by a few paragraphs about each of the three major groups: positive, negative, and neutral.

References to Wine

58 Use accepted as normal part of culture

32 Symbolic (the wine of his wrath, etc.)

27 Wine called a blessing from God

24 Use in offerings and sacrifices

19 Loss of wine an example of a curse from God

16 Examples of abuse of alcohol

15 Vows of abstinence

13 Warnings against abuse

9 Gifts between people

5 Comparisons (x is better than wine)

3 False accusations of drunkenness

3 Rules for selecting deacons

3 Miscellaneous

1 Abstinence in deference to weak consciences

228 Total

References to Strong Drink

6 Vows of abstinence

4 Warnings against abuse

3 Examples of abuse of alcohol

1 Use accepted as normal part of culture

1 Symbolic (the wine of his wrath, etc.)

1 Use in offerings and sacrifices

1 Loss of wine an example of a curse from God

1 False accusation of drunkenness

1 Miscellaneous

19 Total

Summary of References to Alcohol in Scripture

To further distill the verses into a clear view, I divided the 247 references into positive, negative, and neutral references.

Negative

I considered warnings against abuse (17), examples of abuse (19), guidelines for selecting leaders (3), and a warning against causing a brother to stumble (1) to be indications of the negative aspects of drinking. There were 40 such references, 16 percent of the verses.

Positive

I considered examples of the commonly accepted practice of drinking with meals (59), the abundance of wine as an example of God's blessing (27), loss of wine and strong drink as an example of God's curse (20), use of wine in offerings and sacrifices (25), wine used as a gift (9), and metaphorical references as a basis for a favorable comparison (5) to be positive references. There were 145 such references, 59 percent of the verses.

Neutral

I considered the symbolic references, such as the wine of his wrath, etc. (33), vows of abstinence (21), people falsely accused of being drunk (4), and four others that didn't seem to fit in any category to be neutral. There were 62 such references, 25 percent of the verses.

Positive References to Alcohol in Scripture

After I compiled all the numbers and categorized them, the first thing that leaped out at me was the fact that 59 percent of the references were positive. I'd never heard a positive sermon on wine and did not expect this outcome. In fact, I wasn't sure what to make of it at first glance.

Regular Use of Wine

Surprisingly, by far the most numerous type of references to wine in the Bible (58 references, 25 percent) are casual references to wine as an integral, commonly accepted part of the culture. No value judgment is attached to it any more than we would attach a value judgment to a choice of iced tea or Diet Coke with a meal.

I was intrigued that in the minds of the writers of the Bible, no stigma is associated with the casual use of alcohol. Nowhere in these references is it even remotely suggested that it was considered a sin.

It reminded me of a story (likely apocryphal) that I heard about a Baptist preacher who went to Europe for a conference and stayed in the home of a local pastor. He respectfully abstained from the regular use of wine at meals, but he was dismayed. He didn't want to offend, but he felt it was his Christian duty to admonish his brother on the last day of the conference. However, before he had the chance, the European pastor pulled him aside and shared his concern regarding the unhealthy caffeine addiction of the Baptist preacher based on watching him drink several cups of coffee a day during his stay.

An Example of God's Blessing

Back to the verses, as if to pile on my confusion, almost as many times (47 references, 19 percent) an abundance of wine is used as an example of God's blessing, and a lack of wine is used as an example of God's curse. In these references, wine is included along with milk, wheat, corn, children, oil, sheep, cattle, fowl, rain, silver, and gold as blessings that come from God.

This did not fit my expectations in the slightest, but it did make me think of what Paul said about money.

> The love of money is a root of all kinds of evil. 1
> Timothy 6:10

Seeing this verse in the light of verses equating money with God's blessing, I thought I might be seeing a parallel. It's not money itself that is evil, but rather evil comes from the behavior of those who have elevated money beyond its proper position. Was the same true of wine? I set this thought aside for future consideration and continued through the list.

Use in Sacrifices

There are 25 references (11 percent) to instructions or examples of the use of wine in offerings and sacrifices. I wondered how, if drinking wine was a sin, it could be used in sacred rituals. And then there was the detail that Jesus himself continued the Passover tradition by including wine as an essential part of the only sacrament he himself established— Communion.

Do this in remembrance of me. Luke 22:19

I felt the rumblings of a great ship changing course. I had begun this enquiry half expecting the results to confirm the teachings of my childhood, and the Bible itself was challenging those teachings. But I suspended judgment until I saw the whole picture. I was in this to find the truth of the whole counsel of Scripture, and I was only halfway through.

Other References

In the positive section, there are fourteen more verses. Nine times wine is mentioned as a gift (along with things like bread, cattle, and sheep), and five times in the Song of Solomon it is used as a basis for favorable comparisons, such as "thy love is better than wine."

I wasn't through yet, but I was definitely challenged.

Neutral References to Alcohol in Scripture

I found many verses that don't seem to contain any particularly positive or negative connotation. They don't characterize wine as being good, but neither do they contain warnings about the dangers posed by wine. These verses came mainly in two categories.

Symbolic References

There are thirty-two symbolic references to wine, used primarily in reference to acts of God or human behavior that is similar to the effects of wine, such as:

> They, too, will drink of the wine of God's fury, which has been poured full strength into the cup of his wrath. Revelation 14:10

> I am like a drunken man, like a strong man overcome by wine, because of the Lord and his holy words. Jeremiah 23:9

Most of these verses could be used as examples of the prevalence of the everyday use of wine, since symbolism frequently draws from familiar images, which would place them in the positive category, but it seems more appropriate to consider them as neutral.

Abstinence

There are twenty-one references to vows of abstinence that can be separated into two categories: partial abstinence and total abstinence.

One example of partial abstinence includes the case of Levitical priests who were prohibited from drinking wine before going into the temple to perform their duties. However, it is clear that they weren't required to abstain completely since offerings of wine were included along with grain and other goods to financially support the priesthood.

16

This seemed to me like a case of not drinking on the job, which is not the same as a rule against all drinking. It's just a good idea, no matter what you do for a living.

By contrast, the Nazarite vow included a vow of total abstinence from wine and strong drink, along with other signs of being set apart, such as not cutting the hair. In fact, a Nazarite abstained from anything related to grapes, including unfermented grape juice, fresh grapes, and even raisins. This vow was taken by few people and was certainly not something expected of the average person.

The other example of total abstinence is a reference to the sons of Jonadab, who made a vow to their father that they would never drink wine. Jeremiah (a prophet of God, no less) attempted to persuade them to drink wine, but they remained true to their vow. According to the commentaries, the sons of Jonadab were used by Jeremiah as a symbol of faithfulness, a quality that the nation of Israel had lost.

As I considered the vows of abstinence recorded in the Bible, it seemed to me that they were special cases that did not apply to the general population. I put them in the neutral category because abstaining from alcohol for the sake of a vow does not imply that the common use of alcohol is a sin, any more than the Nazarite vow to not cut the hair implies that cutting hair is a sin.

Other References

Bringing up the end of the neutral category, there are four references to people falsely accused of being drunk: three for Hannah and one at Pentecost. These could possibly be considered negative references, but since there are so few (less than 2 percent), their placement is not important. There are also four references that don't seem to fit a category at all. This number is also too small to significantly affect the outcome.

Negative References to Alcohol in Scripture

Of course, it is the negative references that require the most scrutiny. As I looked at them, I discovered something of interest.

All but one of the forty negative references to alcohol in the Bible concern the abuse of alcohol. There are seventeen warnings against abusing alcohol, nineteen examples of people abusing alcohol, and three guidelines for selecting leaders. The three references to selecting leaders caution that those who abuse alcohol should not be selected as leaders. They use the phrases "not given to drunkenness" (1 Timothy 3:3), "not indulging in much wine" (1 Timothy 3:8), and "not given to drunkenness" (Titus 1:7).

As these are warnings against abuse, they seemed to indicate that total abstinence is not required or expected of leaders. Given the number of leaders I know who practice total abstinence, I was surprised with this finding.

By the time I had come to this point in my research, I sensed a fairly clear picture of the larger sort. Based on the content and number of positive references to alcohol and these thirty-nine negative references, it seemed to me that the scriptural position is an emphasis on moderate use of alcohol with a caution against drunkenness.

But one verse remained, and it was a biggie. It was the verse I heard throughout my childhood and beyond in reference to drinking. Before I came to a final conclusion, I had to give full consideration to the remaining reference to wine.

The Weaker Brother

From the standpoint of Scripture, there is one final verse to deal with, and it's a big one, the one dealing with the weaker brother. First, we need to establish what Paul means by a weaker brother.

Let's establish what it is not. The weaker brother is not someone who has a weakness for alcohol. This phrase does not refer to an alcoholic. The Bible has a term for this kind of person, and it's not the weaker brother; it's the drunkard. The weaker brother is not a binge drinker or someone who sometimes has a few too many.

There is more to say regarding the drunkard, to use the KJV term, or the alcoholic, to use a more modern term, that we will cover in the chapter on the law of love. But for now we need to clearly understand that the term weaker brother has nothing to do with abusing alcohol.

As we shall see, the weaker brother is someone with a weak conscience.

What Is a Weak Conscience?

To understand this last and crucial verse, we need to understand the biblical definition of a weak conscience. But before we investigate, consider the following question:

> How would you define a weak conscience? Describe
> the behavior of a person who has a weak conscience.

When I thought of a weaker brother, certain images came to mind, and all involved someone who was weak when resisting temptation. I thought of the words of Jesus to the disciples when they could not stay awake for one hour, something that always made me feel guilty because who can pray for an hour without falling asleep? Certainly not I! Jesus told them:

> Watch and pray so that you will not fall into
> temptation. The spirit is willing, but the flesh is
> weak. Matthew 26:41

That was the image I had of a weaker brother. Imagine my surprise when I dug into that question and found that the Bible established a different definition of weakness—that it in fact defined an interesting

19

(and surprising to me) relationship between a weak conscience and legalism.

The references in the Bible to people whose conscience is not working properly describe, not people who fail to realize they are sinning but people who think they (or others) are sinning when they aren't.

In reference to eating meat sacrificed to idols, Paul says:

> Eat anything sold in the meat market without raising questions of conscience, for, "The earth is the Lord's, and everything in it." If an unbeliever invites you to a meal and you want to go, eat whatever is put before you without raising questions of conscience. But if someone says to you, "This has been offered in sacrifice," then do not eat it, both for the sake of the one who told you and for the sake of conscience. I am referring to the other person's conscience, not yours. For why is my freedom being judged by another's conscience? If I take part in the meal with thankfulness, why am I denounced because of something I thank God for? 1 Corinthians 10:25-30.

The man who has problems with his conscience is the one who is worried about eating the meat, not the one who realizes there is no sin in eating the meat.

This was a stop the presses moment for me! The guy with the weak conscience is the guy who is hung up about what he should or should not do. For someone in an environment who took to heart Psalm 139, it was unsettling.

> Search me, O God, and know my heart; test me and know my anxious thoughts. See if there is any offensive way in me, and lead me in the way everlasting. Psalm 139:23-24

This is a good prayer for any follower of Jesus, and I took a closer look at it. It says, "Know my heart." This resonates with the emphasis of Jesus on the heart rather than on the outward manifestations of following the letter of the law but failing to honor the intent. I saw a connection with Paul's words about eating and drinking.

In Romans, Paul uses the term "weak faith" rather than "weak conscience," but the principle is the same.

> Accept the one whose faith is weak, without quarreling over disputable matters. One person's faith allows them to eat everything, but another, whose faith is weak, eats only vegetables. Romans 14:1-2

Verses 3 and 4 caution each not to condemn the other, both the one whose faith allows him to eat everything and the one whose faith is weak and only eats vegetables.

> The one who eats everything must not treat with contempt the one who does not, and the one who does not eat everything must not judge the one who does, for God has accepted them. Who are you to judge someone else's servant? To their own master, servants stand or fall. And they will stand, for the Lord is able to make them stand. Romans 14:3-4

In perhaps the most severe passage, Paul tells Timothy that people whose consciences have been seared abandon the teaching of the faith and start to teach a legalistic abstinence.

> The Spirit clearly says that in later times some will abandon the faith and follow deceiving spirits and things taught by demons. Such teachings come through hypocritical liars, whose consciences have been seared as with a hot iron. They forbid people to

marry and order them to abstain from certain foods, which God created to be received with thanksgiving by those who believe and who know the truth. For everything God created is good, and nothing is to be rejected if it is received with thanksgiving, because it is consecrated by the word of God and prayer. 1 Timothy 4:1-5

Titus also contains a scathing passage on this topic, which includes this verse.

To the pure, all things are pure, but to those who are corrupted and do not believe, nothing is pure. In fact, both their minds and consciences are corrupted. Titus 1:15

So I found that the weaker brother is the one who sees prohibitions where God has not placed them. Legalism is actually the result of a weak conscience, not a strong conscience developed from spiritual maturity.

Now that we have a better understanding of the context, let's return to the remaining reference to wine.

Better Not To Do Anything

It is better not to eat meat or drink wine or to do anything else that will cause your brother to fall. Romans 14:21

When I read this verse, I realized it was the verse that mattered. Not that the previous 246 verses were meaningless. True, I had detected a certain momentum in the other verses that led me in a surprisingly clear direction, but this seemed to sum things up in the same way that Jesus did when the Pharisees tried to trap him with the question, "Which is the greatest commandment in the Law?" He answered:

> "'Love the Lord your God with all your heart and
> with all your soul and with all your mind.' This is the
> first and greatest commandment. And the second is
> like it: 'Love your neighbor as yourself.' All the Law
> and the Prophets hang on these two commandments."
> Matthew 22:37-40

When I considered Paul's words in context, I saw that he was arguing the same principle, the law of love. Do nothing that would cause your brother to fall.

It didn't matter that 59 percent of the verses were positive references to drinking wine. Truth is not up for a majority vote. This verse could not be ignored or avoided on the grounds that 246 to 1 are great odds. I knew I must face it squarely and consider all the implications. My goal was to find truth, not to justify or discredit a particular bias or denominational position. So once again I dug deeper.

This verse is divided into two parts: (1) a list of things that should be avoided and (2) why they should be avoided. Let's take the second half first.

That Will Cause Your Brother to Fall

If we take a look at the context of this verse, we discover that causing a brother to fall does not mean causing him to specifically eat meat or drink wine. It means to cause him to violate his conscience by imitating an action that he believes in his heart is wrong.

> But whoever has doubts is condemned if they eat,
> because their eating is not from faith; and everything
> that does not come from faith is sin. Romans 14:23

If a weaker brother thinks that drinking wine is a sin, but he sees us drinking wine and decides to drink some himself, still believing in his heart that it is sin, according to this chapter we have caused him to stumble.

This is what Romans 14:21 says we must not do. This is serious stuff. But it doesn't necessarily say what some people try to use it to say.

Some people reference this verse in the King James Version, which says:

> It is good neither to eat flesh, nor to drink wine, nor any thing whereby thy brother stumbleth, or is offended, or is made weak. Romans 14:21 KJV

Most likely any of us who have been Christians for very long have come across someone who has attempted to modify our behavior based on the claim that what we do offends them. These people interpret the word "offended" to mean "an insult or affront."

Based on this interpretation, which is not supported by the context, some use this verse to say, "If you know I am opposed to any use of alcohol and you drink alcohol in spite of that, you have offended me in violation of Romans 14:21."

But an honest reading of the entire chapter makes it clear that verse 21 doesn't say that we have offended a brother if a self-righteous Pharisee feels insulted that we would transgress his cultural interpretation of Christian behavior. We have offended our brother only if we cause him to violate his conscience by imitating actions he believes in his heart are wrong.

The most prevalent interpretation of this verse is more reasonable, frequently using a scenario like the following.

> Christian A picks up a six-pack of beer in the store and buys it. Christian B sees A in the checkout line with the beer. Christian B has been taught from his youth that beer is the drink of the devil and to drink it under any circumstances is sin. However, he is

emboldened by the example of Christian A to buy some himself and drink it, even though he is still convinced in his heart that what he was taught at his mother's knee is true, that drinking beer for any reason is a sin.

Some advance this scenario as the type of situation Romans 14:21 is talking about. They conclude that a responsible implementation of the verse is never to buy or drink alcohol on the off chance that a weaker brother might imitate us and consequently violate his conscience.

I have heard and read this interpretation many times, but as I considered this verse and this scenario, it didn't seem to me to be a reasonable interpretation.

It Is Better

In Romans 14:21, there are three specific actions we are told to avoid if they would cause our brother to stumble. They are:

1. Eat meat
2. Drink wine
3. Do anything else

There's not much in the way of wiggle room in this verse. If it isn't covered in number 1 or 2, then number 3 wraps it up quite neatly. Let's go back and pick up the list at the top, addressing the eating of meat, which we have thus far skipped over, although it has come up a few times.

There are denominations, such as the Seventh Day Adventists (SDA), that recommend vegetarianism and Levitical dietary rules. Many Christians don't agree with this doctrine of the SDA, but the SDA is considered a Christian denomination. Therefore we must consider the Adventists our brothers.

According to the interpretation of Romans 14:21 advanced in the last section, if there is a chance that an Adventist will see us eating pork ribs or a nice breakfast of bacon and eggs and think in his heart, "Hey, sure it's a sin, but just one can't hurt," and join in, we have caused him to stumble. There doesn't seem to be any way around this conclusion if we are going to honestly apply this verse in a consistent fashion.

This application of the verse poses a problem for those who take the Bible seriously. If we truly believe this interpretation to be the accurate one in reference to wine, we are faced with the mandate of restricting ourselves to Old Testament dietary laws in order to avoid causing a brother to stumble.

Going beyond diet, let's consider number 3, doing "anything else that will cause your brother to stumble." Some denominations believe that watching plays and movies, regardless of rating, is a sin. Will we all agree to never attend a movie or play again, or to watch only the news and educational programs that don't involve dramatizations on the television? If not, what happens when someone who believes it is a sin decides to attend a movie because he saw us doing it?

Some denominations believe it is a sin to wear makeup. Will we all agree to forgo makeup? Some denominations believe it is a sin for women to cut their hair or wear jeans. Will we all conform to this regulation on the off chance that we might be imitated by someone who really thinks she shouldn't do these things? What about wearing shorts, mixed bathing, wearing jewelry, buying anything on Sunday, playing cards, playing dominos, listening to James Taylor, using Celtic words for bodily functions instead of Latin words? The list goes on and on.

Practically every part of our culture that we take for granted is considered a sin by some segment of Christianity. Are we prepared to alter every aspect of our behavior in deference to weaker brothers who have problems with things we do every day?

More importantly, is this really what Romans 14:21 is saying? Even more importantly, is this the way Jesus taught and lived his life?

Did he take pains to avoid "offending" the legalistic religious leaders of his day?

This interpretation of Romans 14:21 is not only impossible to apply consistently, it seems at variance with the life and example of Jesus.

A more reasonable interpretation is that if you know someone who believes something is wrong but is tempted to do it anyway, you should abstain for the sake of that person. Otherwise, we would have to live in constant apprehension that some completely innocent action might be imitated by a complete stranger and thus find us in violation of this verse.

Analysis of Scripture: Conclusions

After going through all 247 verses addressing alcohol, it seemed to me that the scriptural position is an emphasis on moderate use of alcohol with a caution against drunkenness. It was not what I was expecting when I began my study, but I didn't see how I could honestly say that the Bible teaches that drinking wine is a sin.

THE EXAMPLE OF JESUS
But I didn't stop there. I decided to take a look at the ultimate role model for a Christian, Christ himself. After all, Paul said:

> Follow my example, as I follow the example of Christ. 1 Corinthians 11:1

And Peter said:

> To this you were called, because Christ suffered for you, leaving you an example, that you should follow in his steps. "He committed no sin, and no deceit was found in his mouth." 1 Peter 2:21-22

In my opinion, at no time should a Christian feel uncomfortable following the example of Jesus. When a doctrine emerges that causes us to ignore or even repudiate the example of Jesus or to imply that Christians cannot use the behavior of Jesus as a reliable guide, it is time to question the doctrine.

I realized that several of the references to wine in the Bible involve Jesus. It seemed to me that to suggest that any use of wine is a sin would be to suggest that Jesus sinned. But as I was growing up, I heard several arguments that addressed this issue.

Was It Really Wine?

Some say that the wine of the Bible was nonalcoholic. In other words, the contention is that when the Bible says "wine," it really means "grape juice." But I wondered about the seventeen warnings against drunkenness and the abuse of wine in the Bible. How did the partakers of the Lord's Table at the church of Corinth get drunk on grape juice? Why would Paul say, "Be not drunk with wine"?

Some say that the wine of biblical times may have been alcoholic, but the alcoholic content was so low that it doesn't compare with the wine of today. But the same questions apply. Whatever the alcoholic content of the wine of Bible times, it was at a sufficient level to require warnings against drunkenness. And what of the twenty references in the Bible to people actually getting drunk?

As I researched the verses, I had to conclude that when the Bible says "wine," then that is exactly what it means.

However, I performed this research in the days before Amazon. com went public, back when information was not as readily available as it is today. Since then several books have been published on the subject, many of them in the first decade of the twenty-first century. See the bibliography for a list I have compiled so far.

As I said in the introduction, I am not a biblical scholar. I don't know Hebrew, Greek, or Latin. Heck, as a Texan, I barely know English. Many experts have written many words analyzing the original languages and the words translated as "wine" and "strong drink" in the King James Version of the Bible. According to the scholars, in the Old Testament two words are translated as "wine," tirosh and yayin. But the scholars often disagree with each other very strongly about how to parse the original language in ways that invalidate each other's arguments.

Some scholars say that tirosh always means "grape juice" and yayin sometimes means "wine" and sometimes means "grape juice." This distinction in the usage of these two words is very important to their argument that the Bible teaches total abstinence.

Other scholars say that both words can mean either "wine" or "grape juice" and that those who teach otherwise are seriously wrong. This usage of the two words is very important to their argument that the Bible teaches total abstinence.

In addition, there is the method whereby they determine how to translate an ambiguous word, which basically comes down to this:

- We will search the original language to see the attitude of the Bible toward drinking fermented drinks.
- This word sometimes means "wine" and sometimes "grape juice." How can we tell how to translate it in this particular verse?
  - o If it's a negative reference, it refers to wine.
  - o If it's a positive reference, it refers to grape juice.

You don't have to be a logician to see the problem with this methodology.

All these issues notwithstanding, any serious student of the topic should take the time, as I have done, to look at their research and conclusions, since they obviously have an advantage when it comes to languages.

What Happened at the Wedding at Cana?

Early in the ministry of Jesus, before he had attracted big crowds and the rancor of the religious establishment, he attended a wedding with his mother. Consider the scene in John 2.

> It's a big celebration. The party has been drinking wine to the point that the host has completely run out and is on the verge of embarrassment. But it's not because he didn't stock enough. The guests have

not restricted themselves to a few discreet sips in a toast to the bride. It is clear from the account that they have been engaged in some serious celebration because they have reached the point where they won't recognize the difference between a good wine and an indifferent wine. In other words, they are at least tipsy. And then Mary asks Jesus to do something about the problem.

I was in my thirties before I attended a wedding where alcohol was available at the reception. The crowd I hung with didn't do wine or champagne at the reception. They probably wouldn't have attended a wedding reception where wine was flowing freely and the drinking was as concerted as is indicated in this story. If they did, they wouldn't have stayed long.

But if my crowd had gone to such a wedding and had stayed to this point in the reception, what would be the probable response when asked to provide more wine for guests who are already drunk? It is unlikely that we would have agreed to replenish the supply, by means natural or supernatural.

Jesus, however, not only replenished the supply, he made an additional six jars, which according to the commentaries held twenty to thirty gallons. So Jesus provided 120 to 180 gallons of wine to a party that was well along the way to inebriation! When I dug deeper into this passage, not only did it contradict everything I had ever heard, it caused me to re-evaluate the conventional understanding of the proper limit of drinking.

Was Jesus a Drunkard?

The second reference to wine in connection with Jesus comes in the form of a false accusation from Pharisees, recorded by Luke.

> For John the Baptist came neither eating bread nor drinking wine, and you say, "He has a demon." The Son of Man came eating and drinking, and you say, "Here is a glutton and a drunkard, a friend of tax collectors and sinners." Luke 7:33-34

Jesus maintains that the Pharisees wouldn't be satisfied regardless of what he did. John the Baptist was a Nazarite from the womb and as a result didn't drink wine.

> For he will be great in the sight of the Lord. He is never to take wine or other fermented drink, and he will be filled with the Holy Spirit even before he is born. Luke 1:15

The Pharisees accused John of having a demon. Notice that the Pharisees didn't twist the truth of John's behavior. It was known that John, as a Nazarite, didn't eat bread or drink wine. However, they slandered John with their conclusion that he had a demon. The Pharisees, evidently astute twisters of the truth, had to have some substance to work with instead of making up things out of whole cloth.

Jesus did not take the Nazarite vow, but ate and drank openly and freely, so they accused him of being a glutton and a drunkard. It seems to follow that in this case their premise was also based on fact, that Jesus ate and drank, but their conclusion was slander.

If Jesus didn't drink actual wine with a significant alcohol content, the charge of being a drunkard would have been too ridiculous to offer. Jesus evidently drank wine to the extent that his enemies thought they could discredit him by spreading rumors that he was a drunkard.

What About the Lord's Supper?

The third reference to wine in connection with Jesus is the sacrament he instituted during Passover, the Lord's Supper, as recorded in Matthew 26:27, Mark 14:23, and Luke 22:17. In all three references the word wine is not mentioned. Instead it says, "He took the cup." However, the occasion was the Passover, and wine is the traditional drink for that celebration. In fact, according to some sources, the Passover tradition of the first century required participants to drink four cups of wine.

As I did my research, it seemed that if the use of wine were truly sinful, it is unlikely Jesus would have used it as a foundational and ongoing ritual of the New Covenant.

The Example of Jesus: Conclusion

While examining the three references to wine in the life of Jesus, I discovered that he did not condemn the use of wine in celebration, that he evidently drank wine as a regular part of meals, that he had little regard for the criticism of the legalistic religious leaders of his day, and that he made wine a primary symbol in the new covenant.

These verses from the life of Jesus reinforced my impression from investigating the 247 references to alcohol found throughout the Bible. It seemed to me that the scriptural position on alcohol is an emphasis on moderate use of alcohol, a conclusion for which I was not prepared.

ALCOHOL AND The Conservative Christian **Subculture.** Most Christians who insist that a Christian must abstain from alcohol are found in conservative Protestant Christian denominations. In these denominations it is not uncommon to hear sermons against any drinking, usually accompanied by statistics like the ones listed in the introduction to this book. The tragedy of these statistics remains, regardless of the analysis of the biblical position. It could be these statistics that lead many prohibitionists to grope for justification in imposing as a biblical mandate what has been discovered to be a cultural preference.

Church History

As more works on the topic of drinking and the church became available in the last few decades, I awaited a book documenting the attitude of the church toward alcohol through the millennia. The closest I have found is *Drinking with Calvin and Luther* by Jim West, noted in the bibliography. However, Jim's book starts with Martin Luther and the Reformation, so it doesn't speak to the previous fifteen centuries.

First there is the period between the life of Jesus and the emergence of the organized, hierarchical church. I haven't found any sources for the church position on alcohol during this time. Then there was the one official, hierarchical church until the split between East and West in the eleventh century, which resulted in the Roman and Greek branches.

Of course, the monks are famous for developing the art of viniculture, brewing beer, and even innovating champagne. But that is not to say that in earlier times attitudes were not different.

Then came the Reformation, starting with Luther and his contemporaries in the fourteenth century. As Jim West clearly documents, the fathers of the Reformation were avid oenophiles and beer connoisseurs.

Because of Jim West, I stumbled upon one detail that astounded me, the story of Elijah Craig. Born in Virginia before the American Revolution, he was ordained as a Baptist minister in 1771. He had conversations with James Madison about how to guarantee religious freedom in the Constitution.

After persecution from the Anglican establishment, Craig left Virginia in search of religious freedom and migrated to Kentucky, where he donated land for the founding of Georgetown College, the first Baptist college founded west of the Allegheny Mountains. He also built a textile mill, a paper mill, a lumber mill, and a gristmill. Craig was evidently an industrious fellow, the very embodiment of the Protestant work ethic.

Then, in 1789, he founded a distillery. He is known as the inventor of bourbon whiskey, being the first to age the locally made corn liquor in charred oak casks.

Did you catch that last detail? A Baptist minister invented bourbon. Most Baptist ministers I have known, and I have known quite a few, have never even tasted bourbon, even though it was invented in the eighteenth century by a Baptist minister.

A century later the temperance movement had taken hold. In these present times, a Baptist minister will likely not have a church left to serve if it becomes known that he drinks bourbon, much less if he owns a distillery. It seems that in the nineteenth century a sea change occurred in the attitudes of the church. That brings us to where we are today, a time when a book like this is necessary.

But Things Are Different Now

Some maintain that alcohol causes much more damage to modern society than ever before, that technology has allowed the effects of alcohol to become vastly more destructive than in biblical times. Because of this increase in social damage, some argue that total abstinence is the only responsible position.

But we must recall the original intent of this investigation. This assertion does not remove the position from the realm of the cultural to the realm of the scriptural. In addition, this claim raises an obvious question. Where is the evidence that shows that a smaller percentage of the population abused alcohol in biblical times? It is doubtful that such evidence exists. It is likely nothing more than an assumption.

More importantly, this is a dangerous argument because it opens the door to relativism. It goes back to the question of scriptural versus cultural principles. Sin is a moral entity, not a cultural one. The final arbiter for the definition of sin is the Word of God, not a personal reaction to the excesses of our society.

Most conservative Christians would agree with the statement that if something was a sin in Jerusalem in AD 30, it is a sin now. In fact, they use this position to oppose attempts to rewrite the Bible to accommodate cultural decadence. Some people want to eliminate sins from the list due to cultural changes, seeking to legitimize adultery or other sins by claiming that the Bible is not relevant to modern social mores. Conservative Christians have rightfully resisted these attempts.

However, if we truly believe that sin is moral, not cultural, then not only must we resist the temptation to drop our favorite sins from the list, we must also resist the temptation to add our current cultural problems to the list. We must admit that the converse of our axiom is also true: If something is a sin now, it was a sin in Jerusalem in AD 30.

Since the Bible doesn't suggest that all use of alcohol was a sin during biblical times, how can it be now?

Jesus was much more critical of religious people adding prohibitions to the burden of the common man than he was of sinners.

> They tie up heavy, cumbersome loads and put them on other people's shoulders, but they themselves are not willing to lift a finger to move them. Matthew 23:4

> Jesus replied, "And you experts in the law, woe to you, because you load people down with burdens they can hardly carry, and you yourselves will not lift one finger to help them." Luke 11:46

Jesus never called prostitutes, adulterers, or drunkards "vipers." He reserved that term for the religious legalists of his day.

Other Social Problems

Some maintain that almost by default our culture abuses alcohol instead of using it in a responsible manner and that the resulting tragic problems in our society justify treating a cultural prohibition as if it were a scriptural position. This logic does not seem to be compelling, but let's give it a look. We can examine some other modern social problems and see what would happen if we applied this same tactic.

As was mentioned earlier, money is listed (along with children and wine and other things) as a blessing from God, even though Paul said:

> For the love of money is a root of all kinds of evil.
> 1 Timothy 6:10

Certainly our culture abuses money, and that abuse causes countless tragic problems in our society. The economic collapse of the "too big to fail" financial institutions at the beginning of this century is a prime example. However, we don't respond to the abuse of money in our society by preaching total abstinence from money. Instead, we teach scriptural principles for the responsible use of money.

The abuse of sex in this current culture causes enormous social problems. The statistics are staggering.

- 41 percent of children in the United States are born out of wedlock. National Vital Statistics Report December 2010
- The Centers for Disease Control and Prevention estimates that there are approximately 19 million new STD infections each year, which cost the US health care system $16.4 billion annually. CDC, Sexually Transmitted Disease Surveillance, 2009
- AIDS is currently killing two million people per year. UNAIDS November 2010

However, we don't demand a total ban on sex of any kind. To the contrary, we teach scriptural principles of responsible sexual behavior.

So, we see that in the cases of money and sex, the church maintains a scriptural position instead of turning to legalism. Why is it that it doesn't do the same on the question of alcohol?

I question the efficacy of a dogmatic prohibitionist stance. Who is the audience of such an appeal?

- Non-Christians who don't have cultural taboos against responsible use of alcohol view this position as another example of religious fanatics wanting to control the lives of other people.
- Christians with a broader view of the scriptural position on alcohol dismiss it as legalistic nonsense generated by the spiritual descendants of the Pharisees.
- Christians with a prohibitionist position agree with each other.

Ultimately, it seems that such a stance is little more than preaching to the choir.

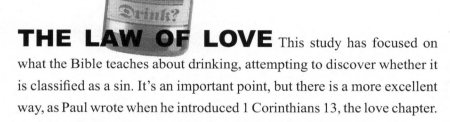

THE LAW OF LOVE

This study has focused on what the Bible teaches about drinking, attempting to discover whether it is classified as a sin. It's an important point, but there is a more excellent way, as Paul wrote when he introduced 1 Corinthians 13, the love chapter.

If we reduce this question to a checkbox on the order of:

Does the Bible say I can do it? Check.

and then brazenly claim our rights when challenged, we've missed the point of the gospel entirely.

The check box is the province of the Pharisee, not the follower of Jesus. It's the primary tool of those who live under the law. If we study the Scriptures to find out what we can get away with, we've fallen into the same ditch as the legalist who studies the Scriptures to find out what he can tell others they can't get away with.

The more excellent way is the law of love, which I first mentioned in the chapter on culture versus Scripture. Jesus mentioned this in another chapter on love, John 13.

> A new command I give you: Love one another. As
> I have loved you, so you must love one another. By

> this everyone will know that you are my disciples, if
>
> you love one another. John 13:34-35

What does this mean for us now that we have come to the conclusion that the Bible does not forbid drinking wine? It means that we do all things guided by the law of love, including drinking wine.

Earlier we talked about the weaker brother and established that Romans 14:21 refers to those with a weak conscience, not to those with a weakness for alcohol. But what about the alcoholic?

In the section on the weak conscience we looked at 1 Corinthians 10:25-30. Now let's look at the two verses that immediately precede it.

> "I have the right to do anything," you say—but
> not everything is beneficial. "I have the right to do
> anything"—but not everything is constructive. No
> one should seek their own good, but the good of
> others. 1 Corinthians 10:23-24

This verse is frequently quoted in discussions about drinking, and for good reason. We can use our liberty to the detriment of others, which violates the law of love.

The Alcoholic

This is where the alcoholic comes into the picture. As it happens, I know a few recovering alcoholics.

About ten years ago I met a guy on a business trip. We kept in touch, and occasionally we would end up in the same town on business and get together for dinner. As I got to know "Bob," I learned that he had traveled into the depths of addiction and out through recovery.

Once when I was in California on business, I went to Bob's house for dinner, and he asked if I would like a glass of wine. I asked if he was sure about that, and he pointed to the well-stocked wine rack in the dining room. He said, "It's not a problem if you drink it; it's a problem if I drink it. You can stop after a few glasses. I can't."

I learned that, like half the people living in California, Bob's wife is a wine aficionado. In fact, I think there's a state law requiring a certain percentage of the population of California to be wine snobs. Bob's wife drinks wine at meals and has for the duration of their marriage. I joined her in a glass of wine. Bob is still sober and strong to this day, despite daily exposure to alcohol.

I don't know an alcoholic who still has a drinking problem, but if I did, I would not place temptation in his path by drinking around him. Yes, I have the biblical liberty to drink, but I choose the more excellent way. I choose to live by the law of love.

For me, it's just a drink. For the alcoholic, it's destruction.

Abstaining for the Sake of Others

I have another friend who frequently comes to my house for dinner parties. "Gustav" enjoys beer and the occasional margarita, but I've never seen him overdo it, not even at the New Year's Eve parties.

As his son grew older, Gustav became concerned about his son encountering peer pressure at school. When his son turned thirteen, Gustav made a covenant with him that neither of them would drink until his son turned twenty-one. When he told me about it at the next dinner party, I asked if he would prefer I not drink. He said, "No, go ahead. You're not the one who made the covenant. I am." Gustav is still holding strong to his vow, even in situations where his son would never know if he had a beer or not.

Gustav is a perfect example of the law of love. He has no misconceptions about what the Bible says about drinking, but he chooses to voluntarily deny himself for eight years for the sake of his son.

In the early days of my marriage, I drank the occasional beer or wine. Although it was over a decade before I did the research for the original version of this document, I felt I had a pretty good sense of the teaching of the Bible on the subject, as opposed to the leanings of the culture in which I lived. We didn't keep beer or wine on hand, mainly because we were absurdly poor and couldn't afford it, but I drank when the occasion presented itself.

One day The Woman came to me and said, "I'm not comfortable with you drinking." She was not raised in a Christian household, but her father was a teetotaler and highly critical of drinking. We talked at length about it, and she agreed that there was no scriptural prohibition against drinking. It was just a personal thing for her. It made her uncomfortable.

My response was, "If it makes you uncomfortable, I won't do it." And I didn't take another drink. We never talked about it. I never asked her for permission to drink at a party. I just quit drinking. As far as I knew, it was forever. There was no expiration date on the vow.

Then one day, ten years later, The Woman came to me on her own and released me from the vow, saying, "You know, I don't mind if you drink. It doesn't bother me anymore." After I verified that she really didn't have a problem with it, I replied, "I'll be right back," and reached for the car keys.

The point here is the law of love, which Paul talks about in the same chapter with the problem verse about the weaker brother, Romans 14. Verse 15 says:

> If your brother or sister is distressed because of what
> you eat, you are no longer acting in love. Do not by
> your eating destroy someone for whom Christ died.
> Romans 14:15

If I ignore something that distresses my wife, what does that demonstrate? That I love drinking more than I love her. If that's true, I should stop drinking anyway because there is a problem, and the problem is not her; it's me.

The Pharisee

Does this mean that if a legalistic abstainer demands that I quit drinking because it distresses him, I will quit? Absolutely not.

That's not an example of the law of love; that's a perversion of the gospel. In fact, in my humble but accurate opinion, it would violate the law of love to validate such behavior. Capitulating to such tactics can only serve to confuse new or weak believers, who could be misled into mistaking such displays of "holiness" with the real thing.

Jesus didn't cooperate with the spiritual bullies of his day who attempted to manipulate and control others through legalism and intimidation. In fact, he reserved his most severe censure for religious bullies, calling them serpents and whitewashed tombs.

As Paul tells us in 1 Corinthians 13, love is patient and kind and does not seek its own agenda. It doesn't steamroll over people, attempting to enforce a viewpoint on others. If I follow the law of love, I will not engage in such tactics and I will oppose those who do.

In fact, it was such a situation that prompted me to do the research on this topic fifteen years ago. I repeatedly endured sermons that equated keeping beer in your refrigerator with murder, rape, and bank robbery. After one sermon too many, I decided to sit down and do the months of research to find the true, full counsel of Scripture.

Before I sat down, I set aside culture, both the prohibitionist doctrine I had been taught from childhood and the impression I had that the doctrine was wrong. I started with a blank slate and a vow to accept the answer regardless of what it turned out to be. Sure, I enjoyed a drink on occasion, but I wasn't beholden to it, as my vow of abstinence years before demonstrated. I was willing to abide by the ruling of Scripture. And I did, although I was surprised at how clear the message was. I expected it to be more ambiguous.

I published the original study as a stake in the ground against legalism and religious bullying. It has resonated with a wide audience, been quoted in magazine articles and books, and been linked to by dozens of websites. In the intervening years, several books have been published on the topic, the majority of them supporting the prohibitionist doctrine. Clearly a book like this one is still needed.

I encourage you to read and discern the Scriptures on this and other topics, and most of all, follow the law of love.

ALCOHOL AND THE BIBLE: Conclusion

Back in the day, I sat down and decided to find out the biblical teaching on the use of alcohol. I read all 247 references to wine and strong drink in the Bible in context to figure this out. I looked at the life of Jesus in the few places where the accounts mention wine. I found a surprisingly simple answer.

The Bible has several warnings against drunkenness, but only one caution against the responsible use of alcohol in celebration and with meals. That caution is to be careful when we are in fellowship with Christians with a weaker conscience. A weak conscience is defined in the Bible as a conscience that sees prohibitions where God has not made them or feels judgment where God has not judged. We are to be careful that we don't cause a brother to stumble.

The one thing I didn't find was a prohibition against the use of alcohol. I leave you with these words from Paul.

> Therefore do not let anyone judge you by what you eat or drink, or with regard to a religious festival, a New Moon celebration, or a Sabbath day. Colossians 2:16

POSTSCRIPT

As I worked through updating this study, I found myself thinking often of my dad. He was a staunch Southern Baptist minister of unimpeachable principles. He was also highly educated, far beyond my attainments. And he would have undoubtedly disagreed with this book, with sound judgment, well-considered words, and impeccable courtesy.

In the beginning of this millennium I had the honor of publishing a set of novels that serve as a testament to his balanced approach to life and Christianity. You can see what others have said about him at BradWhittington.com/father and more information on the novels at BradWhittington.com.

PREVIEW OF
WELCOME TO FRED

BRAD WHITTINGTON

WELCOME TO FRED

{A NOVEL}

CHAPTER ONE

I found it in the back of a drawer in his rolltop desk. Not that I was looking for it. I was just cleaning out the desk. I didn't mind. In fact, I preferred it to cleaning out the closets, which Hannah was doing, or cataloging the furniture, the job Heidi had chosen.

It was a small, black, cardboard ring binder with a white label. The printing on the label was definitely Dad's—a small and precise lettering from a hand that seemed to be more comfortable with cuneiform than the English alphabet. It read: "The Matthew Cloud Lexicon of Practical Usage."

Intrigued, I flipped through it. There were tabbed dividers for each letter of the alphabet. Each page appeared to have a single entry consisting of a word and a definition. I flipped back to the beginning. The first entry was:

> *Adolescence*: Insanity; a (hopefully) temporary period of emotional and mental imbalance. *Symptoms:* mood swings, melancholia, rampant idealism, insolvency. Subject takes everything too seriously, especially himself. *Causes*: parents, raging hormones. *Known cures*: longevity, homicide. *Antidotes*: levity, Valium.

Welcome to Fred

That prompted a chuckle. I had no doubt this entry had been written while Jimmy Carter grinned from the Oval Office. I sat back in the swivel chair for a welcome bit of reflection, which was to be expected, seeing as how we were settling Dad's estate. Nostalgia traps were likely to be rampant in closets and drawers all over the house.

I suppose adolescence is somewhat like insanity. In both cases isolation is sometimes seen as a method for limiting the damage. I suspected that in 1968, when I turned twelve, my parents must have sensed the initial stages of the dreaded malady. I could think of no other reason why they would have moved from metropolitan America to Fred, Texas.

I know you're dying to ask, so I might as well tell you right up front. Fred is located in East Texas, between Spurger and Caney Head. It looks different now, but back then it spanned nine-tenths of a mile between city limit signs and included six buildings of note: a general store, an elementary school, a Baptist church, a hamburger joint, a service station, and a post office. The nearest movie theater was sixteen miles south, in Silsbee. The nearest mall appeared in the early 1970s, forty miles south in Beaumont.

In many ways Fred was idyllic. There was nothing but pine woods and dirt roads to be explored, creeks to be splashed through and swam in, and fresh air to suck into your lungs in an eternal draught. Since I was only twelve and had not yet succumbed to the symptoms of adolescence, I loved it. By the time I hit sixteen, however, Fred's greatest assets had become, for me, its greatest liabilities. There was nothing but pine woods, dirt roads, and creeks.

Still, as a twelve-year-old, I reveled in the unruly semiwildness of the Big Thicket. I delved pine thickets, ferreting out hidden sanctuaries in oil-company tracts, miles from any road. The lust for adventure shared by all young boys provided me with traveling companions.

Swaying one hundred feet in the air at the top of a pine and surveying a green ocean, we were Columbus, devoutly seeking land after months at sea. Cresting the top of a limestone outcrop and finding a bottomless pool in an abandoned quarry, we were Balboa gazing in wonder upon the Pacific. Picking our way through a stagnant bayou, balanced precariously on moss-covered logs and leaping from one knot of ground to another, we were Francis Marion —the Swamp Fox—cleverly eluding the British once again. Following the meandering trail of a dried creek bed, we were Powell winding through the Grand Canyon.

But even in the passion of exploration, caught in the frantic surmise that we were probably the first humans to have ever seen a particular secluded hideout (deduced from the absence of beer cans or other trash), I felt the subtle walls as real as stone between me and my companions.

For example, the names Balboa, Marion, and Powell meant nothing to them. (Of course they knew of Columbus. After all, he had a day named after him to guarantee his immortality.) One of my failings— academic success—didn't endear me to my peers.

Language was yet another plank in the scaffold of my isolation. My parents had taken great pains to weed ungrammatical habits out of their children, with mixed success. In my speech such phrases as "I done did," "I seen him," or "I ain't" were conspicuous by their absence. I discovered that Fredonians didn't trust anyone who talked differently.

But those differences paled against the Great Divider. We had moved to Fred because my father was the new pastor of the Baptist church. I was a preacher's kid (or PK, as we say in the business). Nothing is guaranteed to bring a spicy conversation or a racy joke to a dead halt like the arrival of the preacher's kid. I became as accustomed to seeing conversation die when I approached as a skunk expects the crowd to part when it walks through.

Nonetheless, I tolerated those inconveniences in my preadolescent state, glorying in the remote wilderness like a hermit. It was only when hormonal changes initiated the symptoms of the malady of adolescence that I began to languish rather than glory in my isolation from modern culture. The crude tree house that had served variously as fort, ship, headquarters, prison, hideout, and throne now did duty as a sanctuary of solitude to which I retreated to puzzle out Fred's provincial culture and my place in it.

Many teenage boys would have loved such an environment; indeed, most native Fredonian teens thrived in it. With graceless effort they shot deer, snagged perch, played football, and rattled in pickups down dirt roads. George Jones and Tammy Wynette oozed from their pores like sweat. Under black felt Stetsons they sported haircuts as flat as an aircraft carrier. Pointed boots with taps announced their coming as they approached, and leather belts with names stamped on the back proclaimed their identity as they departed. They dipped snuff, spitting streams like some ambulatory species of archerfish. Their legs fit around a horse as naturally as a catcher's fist nestles in his mitt. They split logs and infinitives, chopped wood and prepositional phrases, dangled fish bait and participles—all with equal skill.

However, in the throes of the teenage condition, I gradually grew dissatisfied with this remote Eden. Although native Texans, our family had spent four years in Ohio. (Since Yankeeland is technically in the same country, no visa or inoculations are required to move there. However, as far as Texans are concerned, Yankeeland is a foreign country and travelers should update their cultural resistance immunization before spending any significant time there.) Nothing can stop the onslaught of adolescence, but perhaps my parents had hoped that my first eight years in Fort Worth were sufficient to inoculate me against Northern influences. Unknown to them, however, I contracted the germs of a companion disease during my four years of Yankee exile.

In the North, I watched in fascination as hippies and flower power bloomed around me. Although too young to participate, I was mesmerized by Peter Max, paisley, and psychedelic posters. Still, I arrived in Fred seemingly intact. But as the symptoms of adolescence surfaced, they triggered the dormant 1960s-counterculture virus, which in turn sprouted in that unlikely Texas garden.

Fred was no place for a would-be flower child seeking sympathetic flora. The British Invasion of the seventeenth century took more than one hundred years to reach East Texas. As I surveyed Fred, I suspected it would take the second British Invasion—the Beatles, the Rolling Stones, and Led Zeppelin—at least that long to reach me.

My distinguishing features, combined with my growing detachment, separated me from the culture short of complete social isolation. Consequently, I remained on the outside looking in, spending most of my teenage years observing rather than participating.

But I guess I should start at the beginning.

CHAPTER TWO In 1964, when Mom and Dad returned to Fort Worth with the news that we were moving to a place where snow stayed on the ground until after Easter, I was skeptical. Who did they think they were kidding? At eight years old, even I knew that snow didn't hang around until April, not even in the Panhandle where they always got snow in the winter. The March ice storm that had accompanied my birth had been a fluke, like the lions whelping in the streets and men on fire strolling through Rome the night before Caesar got it in the neck.

Yet my parents insisted they had actually seen the stuff, right there on the ground. Snow, I mean. Not lions and flaming men. And parents are never wrong.

I wasn't particularly anxious to go north. I felt that living on Felix Street gave me a special connection to Felix the Cat and his bag of tricks, and I was loath to abandon that magical location. Plus, there was a cute girl down the street I wanted to look at a few hundred more times. But, alas, it was not to be.

Heidi didn't welcome the idea either. She was two years older than I was and looked more like Dad—brown hair, green eyes, and tending toward plumpness. Unlike Dad, she was shy and didn't make friends easily. The announcement struck her like a prophecy of exile. No sackcloth and ashes were available at J. C. Penney's, so she had to settle for gloomy looks as she moped around the house.

Hannah didn't share Heidi's outlook. At six years old, she had the inverse apportionment—Mom's looks (slim, blond hair, blue eyes) and Dad's disposition. She looked forward to the trip, her only regret that the snow would be melted before we got there.

As seems to be my lot in life, looking backward at what I was leaving behind left me unprepared for what lay ahead—the change in status from obscurity, as son of a graduate student in theology, to prominence as a preacher's kid. PKs, like preachers themselves, seem to have a spotlight perpetually trained on them, highlighting their every success or failure. But there's one minor difference: preachers are, hopefully, prepared to live in the limelight. Given their choice of careers, perhaps they prefer it.

Somewhere in the seminary curriculum must certainly exist a course explaining that as a member of the congregation an open fly might be noticed by twenty or thirty people, but as the pastor a similar lapse in vigilance in the pulpit will result in hundreds of devout Christians discussing it for weeks, if not years. I suspect the students are required to sign a statement absolving the seminary of all blame in the event of dire embarrassment from undue public exposure. They accept it as part of the territory when they take the gig.

PKs get this fringe benefit with or without prior knowledge or consent. Or signing the form. This gives them plausible deniability, but that is little consolation to those who suffer under a weight that proves too great for many. They break under the strain and tumble into a life of dissipation, taking up bad habits such as spitting and scratching in public or leaving their beds unmade, and they eventually run off to join the circus and fraternize with undesirables such as hurdy-gurdy hustlers and actresses, or other people of that sort.

But my immediate future didn't include actresses, hurdy-gurdies, or even spitting.

The long trek to the North culminated in my first moment in the spotlight. Sunday morning arrived and, as per custom, I found myself in a church. But this was not a large brick building of imposing proportions, with pipe organ, white pews, scarlet carpet, and matching seat cushions. Instead, it was a white nineteenth-century frame building on the edge of downtown, all wood and stained glass, and able to accommodate about three hundred souls, penitent or apostate. Instead of sitting in relative obscurity somewhere in the middle, I sat on the first row in the semigloom. The man in front wasn't some imposing silver-haired gentleman; it was Dad, a pale man, short and dumpy, with a crew cut that made no attempt to disguise the receding hairline, and glasses recovered from the estate of Buddy Holly. He called us up to be introduced. Heidi, Hannah, and I stood in stair-step fashion next to Mom and faced a crowd of perhaps one hundred people who got a good look at us, as though to be able to pick us out in the lineup afterward should there be any trouble.

Little old ladies came by and patted my head and held my hand with their withered claws and told me how cute I was and how happy they were to have the chance to say so. I nodded gravely back at them. Buxom matrons wearing too much powder and perfume hugged me messily and told me how much I looked like my mother. I nodded gravely back at them. Deacons, smelling of aftershave or coffee or cigarettes, slapped me on the back and told me what a fine specimen I was, as if I had been captured and placed in a jar in a natural history museum for their amusement. I nodded gravely back at them. They all had one thing in common: age. Not a kid in sight.

The next day I made the first of many grand entrances into a strange classroom. I didn't encounter much difficulty, other than the fact that all the other kids had learned to write cursive in the second grade, something I was expecting to do in third grade. The teacher dealt with this problem by giving me some books and telling me to figure it out.

The house Dad had located on short notice was a two-bedroom farmhouse, which posed problems for a family of five. I muddled through the third grade with cramped quarters and cramped handwriting. The next summer Dad found a more suitable house in the suburbs, and we moved to another school district. My first day in fourth grade caught the teacher shorthanded when it came to desks. Since I was built along the lines of a soda straw (only with larger hands and feet), she found another slender student and we shared a desk. The other student was a cute girl named Sheila. I approved her plan.

When we finished our lesson, we got a book on birds and leafed through it together, snickering when we got to the picture of two lovebirds. I saw this as an omen, but the next summer our family moved yet again, to a white-flight neighborhood. Just as I was getting around to writing a note that said, "Do you like me? Check a box. ___Yes ___No." (OK, I never said I was quick off the line, but I heard somewhere that slow and steady wins the race.)

I had, by this time, learned how to write at least as well as a doctor. I had also learned that classmates are like the dog that follows you home. Better not get too attached. When a little dark-haired cutie named Carolyn batted her eyes at me, I didn't even have time to organize my note-writing materials before she became the stuff of memory. In September, a two-story frame house opened up in town a few blocks from the church. But the distance from the white-bread-America suburb to the inner-city neighborhood was a lot further than the twenty miles we put on the Vauxhall driving in.

By now, Heidi was in a perpetual state of mourning, which helped me understand the reaction of the Israelites to Jeremiah. I refrained from digging a pit for her, sensing that the plan might not meet with universal approval. Hannah bounced from one school to another with the flexibility of a switch-hitter.

Welcome to Fred

Settling into the house was an adventure. It had a full basement and attic. In my bedroom I discovered the door to the attic stairs. I abandoned unpacking to explore, which I did with the thoroughness of a cartographer. I climbed and crawled over rafters and under dormers, blazing a trail through decades of dust and disintegrating newspapers. I noted the grimy window in the hidden alcove that I claimed, silently, as my personal refuge. It overlooked a mass of housetops and trees with the receding leaf-lines of fall. Next, the basement, which yielded little beyond flaking paint, the smell of mildew, and a monstrous beast Dad identified as the furnace.

The backyard was a rectangle of weeds and crabgrass surrounded by a vine-covered chain-link fence. Dead leaves sloped against the garage. I went to the back fence and peered through the vines. A large set of brown eyes peered back from a dark face. I jumped back, tripped, and fell backward. A strange sound emerged from behind the curtain of leaves. I rolled to my knees and looked through the bottom of the fence.

A Negro boy was rolling on the ground, snorting like a pig and kicking up leaves and dust. Evidently he had also been startled and was having a seizure of some kind. I tried to remember what to do, something about making sure he didn't swallow his tongue. I wasn't sure how to do that, but I assumed time was a critical element. I was halfway over the fence, trying to disentangle my shoelace, when the snorting changed to a thin, rising and falling wail. I paused, puzzled. Obviously he wasn't swallowing his tongue. As I stood in frozen indecision, the noise became a sound that left me both relieved and annoyed. Laughter.

I straddled the fence, shoes crammed pigeon-toed into the wire, glaring with impatience and pique. The convulsions of glee subsided into tremors of giggles, like the fading thunder of a passing storm. I waited, looking down from my exalted position with royal disdain. However, each time the boy looked up at me, the sirenlike noise erupted, and he flopped about on the ground, mottled brown and black, dust on skin.

My ankles complained of the impossible angle I had forced on them. I shifted my weight to my hands, but the vines were too insubstantial to support even my meager weight, and I tumbled into the yard onto the laughing boy. This development, while alarming me, only served to increase his amusement. He suffered a relapse of the snorting stage, rolling around and slapping weakly at me as he laughed.

I struggled to my feet and looked down at him with as much amazement as annoyance. How could he sustain such spasms without internal injury? He grabbed at my leg and used me as a support to crawl to his feet, leaning against me and laughing. Odors of grass, dirt, and the musky smell of the boy's sweat mingled in the air. I felt him quivering as he staggered against me. As if it were spread by contact, I began to be infected by his laughter and, against my will, found myself chuckling. The boy looked up from his bent stance and pawed feebly at my chest, trying to catch his breath between barks of delight. This struck me as rather amusing, and I began to laugh in earnest. We spurred each other on to greater heights of hilarity until we both collapsed on the ground and surrendered to an ecstasy of elation. It gradually faded in fits and giggles, replaced by the contented silence of exhaustion.

I sat up. "Mark," I said, holding out my hand.

"Yes?" He looked at my hand. Bits of grass and leaves adorned his close-cropped hair like Christmas ornaments. Now that we had recovered from our convulsions, I was able to get a look at him. He was very dark, like the dark chocolate Mom liked but none of us kids did. He was a little shorter than I was, and much stockier, which was no great feat. I had seen walking sticks with more meat on their bones than I had. His head bulged out in back as if to counterbalance his large nose and lips. He was wearing a brown V-neck T-shirt under a nappy burnt-orange sweater. Black high-tops protruded from his frayed jeans.

"I'm Mark. What's your name?" My hand hung out between us.

"Marc." He grabbed my hand and shook it as vigorously as he had laughed earlier.

"Right. And you are?" I vibrated from the energy of his handshake.

"Marc." He continued to shake my hand, smiling hugely.

I began to wonder if I had tumbled into the grounds of a private lunatic asylum. I looked at him blankly while developing an appreciation for the rigors of the life of a pump handle.

He finally quit shaking my hand and stood up. "Only youse guys prob'ly spells yours with a K, as in Mark Twain. Mine has a C, as in Marcus. Marcus Malcom Marshall, to be exack, as in Garvey, X, and Thurgood, respectively. No relation, though. But everybody jus' call me M." The torrent of words gushed from him with no discernable pauses for breathing.

I hated to admit I didn't follow any of it. I latched onto the one part I did understand. "M?"

"Yep. Man, you talk funny. Where you from?"

"I talk funny? Youse guys talks funny."

"Alabama? I bet it's Alabama," he declared, undeterred by my comments.

"Alabama?" I snorted in disgust.

"Texas, then."

I was torn between pride at being a Texan and reluctance to admit he had guessed correctly. "Fort Worth," I countered.

"And Bingo was his name-o!" M declared with a quick pirouette of triumph and a short siren wail of laughter that was suddenly cut off. "Come on," he said, grabbing my arm and dragging me away from the fence.

"Where are we going?"

"You gots to meet Mama."

"I do?"

"Yeah, everybody gots to meet Mama."

I looked back at the fence, catching a glimpse of the moving van above the vines. From a second-story window, Hannah peered out through the film of grime on the glass like the ghost in a Gothic novel. I attempted a shrug, which was difficult while being dragged across M's backyard. I waved as we mounted the back steps, but it probably looked more like a kid reaching back toward the house in distress. Then we disappeared through a screen door.

We maneuvered through a dank laundry room and emerged into an amalgam of potent odors. A very tall, slightly plump and very black woman stood in front of a stove. She was wearing an apron over a nice dress. Without turning around she said, "Go back an' wipe your feet. I jus' mopped this floor." I looked down. The linoleum was a dull yellow, cracked and curling, but clean. I was dragged back through the laundry room to the doormat, where M and I wiped our feet and returned to the kitchen.

"Mama, it's Mark from Texas, but with a k, as in Mark Twain." He shoved me forward, and I stumbled to a stop at the foothills of the black mountain towering above me. She turned around, ladle in hand, and smiled down at me with large teeth. "Hello, Mark from Texas." She held out a hand, the pink palm enveloping my puny white hand. "Did you move in back there?" She pointed the ladle toward our house.

I nodded.

"Well thas jus' fine. Careful you don't let M talk your ears off."

I nodded, again.

"Are youse guys hungry?" she asked. I looked apprehensively at the steam rising from the pots on the stove. I had no idea what was in them, but the deep odors didn't call to the deep of my appetite. The aroma verged between a slaughterhouse and a laundry.

M leapt as if he'd been stabbed in the flank with a hat pin. "Yes!" he cried, producing two plates seemingly from thin air. He placed them on the green Formica tabletop. Before I had a chance to say "Pepto-Bismol," I was seated in front of a plate of limp, slimy green leaves and some unidentified meat in a watery brown sauce.

"You comin' from Texas, I'm sure you been havin' some chitlins and collard greens lots of times," Mrs. Marshall said.

"Not that I recall," I replied. I assumed the green stuff was the greens, so the other must be the chitlins.

M looked at me in disbelief, and his mother said, "Well, then, you is in for a real treat!"

I was now on center stage, the audience waiting for my next move. My fork wavered over the plate like a divining rod. I went for the meat. Two sets of eyes followed my fork to my mouth. I chewed quickly and swallowed, and waited for the taste to catch up. Not bad. Pretty good, actually. I enthusiastically went for another bite and made a devoted friend. Mrs. Marshall nodded and turned back to the stove. And not a moment too soon because the greens were another story entirely. I was able to finish them with generous portions of chitlins.

As I was forcing down the last bit of greens, I heard a knock on the back door. Mrs. Marshall disappeared into the laundry room. A familiar voice said, "Good afternoon. I'm Matthew Cloud, just moving in across the way. I was checking up on my son, who I understand might be bothering you folks over here."

Mrs. Marshall laughed. "Oh no, Mr. Cloud, he ain't no trouble. He jus' finishin' up a plate of chitlins and collard greens right now. That boy needs some fattenin' up!"

Dad walked in to see me with a forkful of chitlins suspended between plate and mouth. Hannah, evidently the messenger who had alerted Dad to my abduction, peeked her blond head around the door like a sideways Kilroy.

"Well, I suspect you're right about that point," Dad chuckled, apparently amused at the sight of me tossing down the chitlins like one of the family. "I'm afraid I'm going to have to borrow him back. It's a little matter of a dozen boxes in his room he was supposed to unpack before he took off."

The Amazon clicked her tongue disapprovingly, and I suddenly felt guilty. I gulped down the chitlins and jumped up.

"Thanks." I looked at M. "I guess I have to go back now."

Mrs. Marshall nodded at me. "You're welcome, Mark. And I hope you come back when you done your chores."

I looked at Dad. "Sure, if it's not too late."

Unpacking took until after dark, but Sunday after church I returned. M took me on a tour, starting with a basement much more interesting than mine. Poor lighting, unfinished walls, and exposed rafters gave it the ambiance of a cave. M grabbed a hammer and pounded furiously at a sixteen-penny nail jutting from one of the studs.

"When Papa hits a nail, there's sparks fly," he said with respect, and swung the hammer again. "Hey, I think I saw a spark. Here, you try it, man." I declined, but M wouldn't rest until I had taken a few ineffectual swings at the nail. No sparks.

The rest of the house wasn't much different from mine, albeit in a more advanced stage of disintegration. M's attic view faced the opposite street, so I was able to see how the other half lived as we sat on an old trunk and squinted through the grime. More roofs and trees in their final stages of abandonment.

"That's the school over there." M pointed at a square roof several blocks away. "What grade are you in, man? I bet it's fifth."

"Fifth."

"And Bingo was his name-o!" he cried and attempted a pirouette, but the cramped quarters of the attic made it impossible. He settled for a jig and a chuckle. "Me too. Which class? I bet it's Ma Barker's." He stood poised for another victory dance.

"I haven't been yet."

"Oh, yeah." He sat back down on the trunk. "What's it like in Texas?"

"I don't know. Like here, only no basements. And hotter."

"One day I'll go see. I'm gonna go see everything, like Marcus Garvey."

"Like who?"

"The Right Excellent Marcus Mosiah Garvey." He waited, but I had nothing to say. "Never met the guy," seemed flippant.

"Malcom X?"

I shook my head.

"Thurgood Marshall?"

I shook my head.

M looked at me for a long while with an impassive stare I couldn't interpret, as if he were trying to make up his mind. He suddenly stood up and walked down the attic stairs; I followed him to his room. He pulled a thin paperback book from a cardboard box next to his bed and shoved it at me. I looked at the title: *The Negro Protest: James Baldwin, Malcom X, and Martin Luther King Talk with Kenneth B. Clark.* I looked back up at M, but he just walked past me and down the stairs. We walked through the kitchen to the back door. "I'll see you tomorrow, man," he said and closed the door behind me.

CHAPTER THREE I was indeed in Ma Barker's class, who turned out to be Mrs. Barker, a middle-aged white woman and not, as far as I could tell, the matriarch of a bloodthirsty outlaw gang. But you have to admit, being a fifth-grade teacher would have been a great cover.

After school I found M waiting at the back fence.

"Come on," he said. "It's Meesha and Keesha's birthday."

"Meesha and Keesha?"

"The twins."

"I would have never guessed. What twins?"

"Harriet's twins. Just come on and you'll see."

In the living room a sheet was spread out on the worn wooden floor. In the middle a cake slathered in white icing was graced with a single candle flickering in the drafty room. Two identically dressed babies sat on either side, looking up at the looming adults with that complacent apprehension one sometimes finds in babies.

A girl I took to be Harriet towered over them, and me. She was wearing a purple paisley tube of some kind of stretchy material with a black patent-leather belt. Her large hands and feet left no doubt as to whose daughter she was. She wasn't quite as dark as M, except around her elbows and knees. She hovered over the twins in a half-crouch, her knees together. "Blow out the candle," she said in baby talk. The twins just looked at her.

"Make a wish," Mrs. Marshall said, also in baby talk and also towering. The twins blinked in unison, realigned their sights on her, and picked up where they had left off, doing their best imitation of confused one-year-old babies.

Across the room an older man with close-cropped gray hair sat in a frowzy armchair, a newspaper open in his lap. He watched the babies dispassionately, but I thought I detected a hint of amusement.

M strode forward. "They don't know how to blow out a candle. They're only one!" He leaned over and blew the candle out.

"Now have some cake," Harriet said.

"Yes, eat your birthday cake," Mrs. Marshall said. "It's chocolate. Everybody like chocolate cake."

M looked from his sister to his mother with exasperation, leaned over, scooped icing off the cake with his finger, and shoved some in each baby's mouth. Their expressions changed instantly, and they converged on the cake. Before Mrs. Marshall had time to cut us slices from the other cake set aside in the kitchen, there were three lumpy masses of icing and cake in the middle of the sheet, like an accident scene of a collision with a zebra, a penguin, and a nun. Two of them moved. M and I disappeared into the basement before we were recruited for cleanup duty.

M dug up two claw hammers, turned off the light, and we took turns banging on a nail, trying to make sparks. We labored in shadow, silhouetted by the light from the little rectangular basement window high above us.

I began singing "I've Been Working on the Railroad" but stopped when M threatened to switch his attentions from the nail head to my head.

"Did you read that book I gave you, man?" M asked between strokes.

"Hey, that was only two days ago."

"Do you know who John Brown was?"

I began singing again. "John Brown's body lies a molderin' in the grave . . ." but the silhouette of M's hammer hung over me in the gloom and I quit.

"Why was his body molderin' in a grave?"

"He was dead." That was an easy one!

"Why did he die?"

That was a little tougher. "Uh, chicken pox?"

M rolled his eyes, which was about all I could see of him, and resumed his hammering. "Do you know who George Washington was?"

"Of course."

"George Washington Carver?"

"Yes."

M stopped. "Really?"

"Of course. He invented the peanut." I held the hammer aloft and spun around. "And Bingo was his name-o!"

M didn't laugh. "OK, man, how about W. B. DuBois?"

I stopped and peered at him in the dimness. "Uh, can you spell it?"

"Marcus Garvey?"

"That's the guy you're named after, right?"

"One of them."

"What did he do?"

"Read the book." He slammed the hammer down. "Look, sparks!"

As the weeks passed, M and I eventually bored of banging on nails in the basement and hanging from rafters in the attic. My house offered even less excitement. We had already squeezed the neighborhood dry of every last drop of entertainment. We started making regular Saturday trips to the library, ten blocks downtown.

Sometimes we took detours, exploring sections of downtown. One of our favorite spots was next to the theater, which was in the middle of the block. The parking lot was in the back by the alley, but the entrance was in the front on the street. A long corridor through the building provided a shortcut. It was paved in small, white ceramic tiles, the floor undulating in gentle waves. The sides jutted in and out at sharp angles, with columns against the walls at regular intervals along the way. It was enclosed with a glass door at each end.

The corridor provided a great setting for reenacting episodes of *I Spy,* the old spy show with Robert Culp and Bill Cosby. M thought it was amusing and appropriate that Cosby was the intelligent one in the show. I didn't concur.

We would traverse the corridor, running and ducking behind columns, shooting at imaginary villains or, sometimes, at each other, an inexplicable plot development for which the scriptwriters had not provided. Before long our territory for spying extended down the alley and out several blocks, past the back doors of cleaners, diners, barbershops, and five-and-dimes.

Late one Saturday afternoon, as the shadows were stretching to the horizon, I was eluding M, who stalked me down the corridor. In a bold move I rushed the alley door, almost colliding with a couple on their way to see *Fantastic Voyage.* Their confusion delayed M, allowing me to round the corner before he could see which way I went. I had a plan. I sprinted down a dead-end alley, thinking he would never expect me to trap myself. At the end, I climbed some trash cans and dropped over a dilapidated wooden fence into a neglected area behind an auto shop.

It was the perfect refuge, one I had discovered the week before when I was the hunter instead of the hunted. I planned to crouch along the back fence, watching for M's approach. For cover, I had my choice of a fifty-five-gallon oil drum or a large cardboard box that had once held a washing machine. It lay on its side, old rags spilling out onto the ground. I chose the oil drum, from which I could peek through a knothole in the fence. I checked my surroundings. The asphalt faded a few feet from the shop into dry, cracked, packed dirt broken up with weeds and littered with rusted transmissions, wheels, mufflers, and other detritus. A metal door padlocked on the outside broke the brick wall of the shop, which had been painted white a long time ago. The only other access to this area was a two-foot gap between the shop and the liquor store that ran the length from the alley to the street.

I watched for M's shadow on the bricks of the alley, the rags in the box rustling in the wind. Then I realized there was no wind. I jerked away from the fence and looked at the rags. From the shadow of the box a raspy voice asked, "What's yer name, boy?"

I couldn't have been more startled if the oil drum had started to spontaneously play "Wipe Out." I was poised to jump and run when a face materialized among the rags and shadows. A woman's face. Green eyes burned from sunken wells of eye sockets. A wealth of nascent wrinkles was evident on the leathery skin, skin that had seen many a day in the open sun and more than one night under the stars. Short brown hair, matted and tangled, disappeared into the tattered brown blanket draped around the woman. But what held my eye captive was the large purple-red birthmark that ran from her left eyebrow to her cheek in a meandering splotch.

"Yer name. What's yer name?"

I said, as if in a trance, "Mark."

"Ah, the Mark. The Mark. It's got the Mark." An emaciated hand fluttered to her left temple and dropped down like a bird frozen and falling from a branch.

"Well, Mark, do you have anythin' so much as a fiver on yer?" I shook my head slowly. "I could use a bite to eat, yer know. How 'bout some change?" Her eyes burned even brighter. "I got a powerful thirst." She looked at my pants pocket, the one with the dollar in it, as if she could see it through the fabric. Her hand twitched.

As if on its own, my hand dug down and produced the dollar. I held it out, fluttering from my shaking hand in the stillness. Her hand shot out like a cobra and snagged the bill, eyes flaring up and returning to the burning green.

"Thank ye, thank ye. Mighty white of ye, Mark." A low, raspy chortle emerged from the depths of her throat. She unfolded from beneath the blanket like a moth shedding a chrysalis. A worn and dirty cotton print dress flapped a few inches above her ankles and the worn brown brogans on her feet as she shuffled to the gap and disappeared.

I blinked and felt as if I had suddenly awakened. Had I dreamed it? I reached into my pocket. The dollar was gone. I climbed the oil drum and vaulted the fence into the alley, ready to be found by M.

I didn't tell anyone about the Creature, but I couldn't erase her image from my mind. I dreamed about her Saturday night. Her face of creases and splotches haunted me during the Sunday school lesson of the woman at the well. In church I formulated a plan. When the offering plate went by, I held an empty hand low over the plate and thumped the bottom with the other thumb as it passed in front of me, my money still safe in my pocket.

At home that afternoon I hopped the back fence in pretense of visiting M, but passed his house. Downtown I walked through the tile corridor, turned into the blind alley, climbed gingerly over the fence, and dropped quietly to the ground.

The Creature was in the box, but she didn't acknowledge my presence. I crept closer, alert for any movement. As I approached, I heard a steady raspy sound from beneath the bedraggled blanket. Something clinked on the ground—my foot had hit a clear flask. I kicked it over and looked at the label. Gin. I looked at her a little longer, then threaded my way through the gap to the street.

It took me awhile, but I finally found a place I could buy a sandwich and a bottle of Coke with the offering money. I returned to the box, set the food on the ground, and sat down on a wheel in the shade of the fence. After awhile I got tired of waiting and started throwing pebbles at the box. Three minutes and twenty pebbles later, I was rewarded.

The Creature stirred, saw the food, and looked suspiciously out of the box. The purple splotch was dark against the pale skin on the left side of her face. "It's the Mark," she croaked. She crawled out of the box, snatched the food, and sat on the edge of a transmission housing several yards away, her feet straddling a dirty red stream of transmission fluid.

She positioned herself so she was facing the gap in the wall, but could see me from the corner of her right eye. I watched in silence while she devoured the sandwich like a wild animal, eating some of the paper wrapping in her haste. Once the sandwich was gone, she picked up the Coke and drank the entire bottle slowly in one long draught, looking at me obliquely with leaden green eyes like the Atlantic on a cloudy day. She closed her eyes and let out a belch that reverberated through the courtyard.

In a sudden movement she hurled the bottle against the liquor shop wall. It shattered in a shower of glass and I jerked like I'd been slapped.

"The Mark follered me. What's yer game?"

"Game?"

She turned her head slightly in my direction with a jerk, eyes narrowing and darting, sometimes in my direction, sometimes around the littered courtyard, like a bird watching a cat while looking for food. "Meaty, beaty, big and bouncy." She dropped her chin, lowering her coarse voice until it sounded like a man. "He speaks plain cannon fire, and smoke and bounce."

I looked at her blankly.

She raised her head, voice returning to its normal level, and peppered me with questions. "Got the drop on me? Got me bang to rights? Flushed me out, five by five?"

"I just thought you might be hungry. At least, I remember you saying something like that."

The Creature grabbed the frayed hem of her cotton print dress and wrapped it tightly around her calves, bunching it up in her hand. Brown legs covered with black hair extended to the scarred brogans below.

"The Mark was hungry." She rocked forward and backward on the transmission. "In hunger and thirst," she rasped in a throaty whisper, "in nakedness and dire poverty, ye will be a restless wanderer on the earth. But the Mark will foller ye." She twisted the cloth in her hand and turned her head slowly toward me.

"I was also powerful thirsty." Her eyes followed mine to the empty gin bottle. "Fancy a drink?" I shook my head. "Got another dollar on yer?" I shook my head again. "Didn't reckon yer did." She turned her head back and rested her chin on her knees, keeping watch on me from the corner of her eye. We sat in silence for awhile.

I finally got the courage to speak. "What's your name?"

The Creature didn't move, or even blink, but I heard a small growl that seemed to echo from the walls enclosing us. It could have only come from her, since we were completely alone.

"Lilith," she hissed.

"Thilly rabbit," she lisped in falsetto. She jerked upright. "Thufferin' thuckotash, the Mark follered me!" She looked at me suspiciously. "Yer tryin' to make me?"

"Make you what?"

"Stand and deliver," she boomed, jumping up and stomping in the red mud at her feet. "The Mark follered me. Which one are ye? Senoy? Where are yer friends?" She reached into the neckline of her dress and pulled out a chain with some kind of charm or pendant hanging from it.

It looked like a cross, but the top was a loop. "Sansenoy, Semangelof, show yerselves!" Holding the charm toward the sky, she turned slowly around, looking at the roofs surrounding us. "Yer can't touch the child. I have the Mark!"

I looked around apprehensively. Who was she talking to?

The Creature completed her circle, scowling at the sky. Then she dropped the chain back into her dress, shuffled to the cardboard box, and crawled in, wrapping the blanket around her and facing out so that I couldn't see the purple splotch on her face. "Who are ye?" she whispered. "What do yer want?"

"You know my name but I don't know yours."

"Naamah," she said, hoarsely. "Just call me Naamah."

"Naamah? What kind of name is that?"

"The kind I hand out fer free. I make yer a present of everythin' I said today." She was silent for a few seconds. "What do yer want?"

"I just wanted to find out about you." I ignored the babble. "After all, I did give you a dollar. And some food," I added, in an attempt to shame her into answering my questions.

"And here I thought ye was doin' yer Christian duty."

"Maybe I was. I can still get something for it, can't I?"

"Oh, no. Yer supposed to do it expectin' nothin' in return." She cleared her throat, which induced a coughing fit that concluded in her spitting phlegm four feet in front of the box. In a deep, throaty voice she intoned, "Cast yer bread on the waters. Don't let yer left hand know what yer right hand is about. Ye ask and receive not because yer ask amiss, fer yer own selfish lusts."

After this last utterance, she arranged the blanket low on her shoulders like a party shawl and tossed a suggestive leer my way. Her green eyes sparkled from beneath the shadow of her brow. I saw the ghost of a younger woman—attractive, carefree, a hint of playful innocence.

Then she turned her face full toward me, and I caught sight of the purple splotch. The ghost was exorcised. Her eyes returned to the dull, leaden green I had seen earlier, and she glowered at me.

"What do yer want, boy?" she demanded in a threatening growl.

I glanced around nervously and looked back at her without a word. She turned, crawled into the recesses of the box, and pulled the blanket over her head. I waited for awhile, staring at her brogans, then got up quietly, circumnavigated the box, and squeezed through the gap toward home.

CHAPTER FOUR

The next Saturday M and I made our library trip as usual. I let M use my twenty-inch Spyder bike with the chopper handlebars and tiger-skin banana seat; I "borrowed" Heidi's bike. (I would not have normally agreed to be seen in public on a girl's bike, but it had a large basket convenient for transporting the large number of books we always checked out.)

I was quiet as we rode along, which didn't bother M. He chattered, oblivious to my silence. My thoughts were on the Creature and how she was faring. I wanted to check on her, but I didn't know how to ditch M. As we neared the theater, I made a snap decision, turning down the alley instead of taking the street to the library. It took M awhile to realize I wasn't with him. He stopped in midsentence. "Hey, man, where you goin'?"

"This way," I hollered over my shoulder. He caught up with me at the end of the blind alley.

"Hey, what . . . ," he started, but I held up my hand for silence.

"Wait here," I whispered, "I want to check on something." I climbed the trash can by the fence.

"Where are you going?" he asked in a stage whisper.

I jumped over the fence. The courtyard was unchanged. I padded silently to the cardboard box, but the Creature wasn't there. I stood looking into the box's shadows when M dropped over the fence.

He looked around nervously. "What are you doin'?" he demanded in a hoarse whisper. "Are you crazy?"

I could see something in the back recesses of the box, beyond the tattered blanket, and was intrigued by the thought of what the Creature would stash away. I hoped it might give me a clue to who she was and why she lived as she did. I looked around quickly and dropped down, reaching into the box. A miasma of sweat, alcohol, and vomit enveloped my head and I rolled back out, gasping for fresh air.

M said, "Hey," but I took a deep breath and plunged back in, so I didn't hear the rest. My hand reached back and closed on the object. It was a small Bible, bound in limp, black leather with the name Pauline Jordan barely legible in flaking, gold gilt letters. A screeching wail and a startled shout caused me to drop the Bible, and I scuttled backward like a deranged crab.

M was backing toward the fence, his eyes large and fixed on something behind me. I spun around. The Creature shuffled toward me, a large cabbage nestled in the crook of her arm. The other arm stretched out, forefinger extended toward me like an accusation, trembling.

"The man who does not enter the sheep pen by the gate, but climbs in by some other way, is a thief and a robber," she screeched, spittle in the corners of her mouth. Then she saw my face. "The Mark," she breathed. "The Mark follered me."

Her gaze drifted from me to M. "Ham," she said, eyes burning a deep green. "Cursed be Canaan! The lowest of slaves will he be to his brothers." She jumped a menacing step in his direction, and he disappeared over the fence without a word.

The Creature turned to me. "Those who hate me without reason outnumber the hairs of my head," she said with deep venom and threw the cabbage at me. I dodged it and followed M over the fence. It took me a block to catch up with him. He didn't stop until we were on the steps of the library.

"What was that?" he demanded between gasps for air.

"I think it was Pauline." I told him the story of my previous visits.

He shook his head. "Don't mess with her, man. She's crazy."

Once inside the library, M insisted I get something by "my namesake," so I picked up a copy of *Tom Sawyer* to go with *Treasure Island*. M got *Homer Price* and *The Underground Railroad*. We got on the bikes and headed back. I suggested a detour by the church to watch Dad work on the furnace, a recalcitrant coal-burning monstrosity in need of occasional rehabilitation. We were halfway down the hill to the church, zipping along at a good pace, when my shoelace got hung in the chain. I couldn't pedal forward because the lace was wrapping around the center shaft and binding up. I couldn't pedal backward because the bike had coaster brakes. I had finally figured out that I had to hang my foot out to the side and turn the gears to push the lace through when I heard a yell.

While I had been preoccupied with the physics of shoelace-from-gear removal, I had traveled the half block to the corner, gaining speed all the while. A flash of tiger skin, black skin, and large white eyes passed under me as I mowed M down and lurched into the street—just in time, as luck would have it, to bounce off the side of a passing mail truck turning right. The rear bumper of the truck snagged the front tire of Heidi's bike and dragged me back up the half block to the point where my troubles had begun before the driver realized he had a bike attached to him like a lamprey on a shark. He screeched to a halt, jumped out, and ran back to where I sat, dazed. I was still sitting astride the bike, which leaned toward the front of the truck, held up at a forty-five-degree angle by the bumper. I stared at him, my attention riveted to a patch on his shirt that said, "Dotson."

"What's all this, then?" he demanded.

I was roused from my stupor and leaped backward from the bike. "Oh, no! Oh, no! Oh, no!" I shouted.

"What?" Dotson leaped backward too.

"Heidi will kill me! Look at the bike!" The front tire was shaped like a paramecium, the spokes splayed out like cilia.

"Look at you!" he responded.

I looked down and leaped backward again. "Oh, no! Oh, no! Oh, no!"

"Now what?" Dotson asked as he echoed my leap.

"Mom will kill me! Look at my shoe! I just got these yesterday!" My left shoe looked like it did when I left the store. My right shoe looked like Old Glory after a particularly rough night of shelling. It was in a state unlikely to inspire the most ardent patriot when viewed by the dawn's early light. Viewed by the afternoon's light, it was appalling.

A lady, looking like she was constructed entirely of feather pillows cinched up in an apron, scudded from the house behind us. "Oh my goodness! I saw the whole thing. Are you OK?" she screeched in a flurry of agitation, practically running a figure eight around Dotson and me, her hands pressed to her cheeks, fingers splayed like overstuffed sausages in a pan of dough.

If only her voice had been as soft as she appeared to be. Instead, it had much in common with the screeching of metal on metal I had heard while the truck was transforming Heidi's bike into modern art. She could have had the same effect with a lot less effort if she had just pounded nails into my ears. I covered my ears with my hands.

Dotson thrust his hand in my direction. "He's crazy. He keeps raving about his bike and his shoes."

Mrs. Puffy-Screechy looked at me holding my head. "Oh my goodness, oh my goodness! He hit his head! I must call the ambulance." She veered toward the house and screeched, "Heathcliff! Call an ambulance. He hit his head." Then she spiraled in my general direction, grabbed me, and steered me through the gate to the porch. "Here, you must sit down and don't alarm yourself. No time for hot tea, but I can bring you some lemonade." She disappeared into the house, squeaking, "Oh my goodness, oh my goodness."

I looked around, wondering how I ended up on the porch swing. Dotson produced a little cigar with a white plastic mouthpiece and paced beside the truck, trailing smoke like the Little Engine That Rather Wouldn't. He stopped occasionally to gesticulate toward the bike and ask "Now what?" to nobody in particular.

Mrs. Puffy-Screechy reappeared, thrust a jelly glass into my hand, and disappeared back inside the door like a Frau in a cuckoo clock. I stared at the lemonade. She popped back out again with a wet dishrag and slapped it against my forehead. "Here, hold this on." I was sitting on the swing, lemonade in one hand and a dishrag in the other, when M came running up the sidewalk to the porch, leading Mom, Heidi, and Hannah. I was attempting to explain what had happened, pointing at my shoe with the dishrag—which Mrs. Puffy-Screechy kept pushing back up to my forehead—when an ambulance appeared. The technicians jumped out, popped open the back door, and pulled out a gurney.

"I'm OK. I can walk," I hollered and jumped up from the swing, spilling the lemonade.

"Oh my goodness, oh my goodness, he's going to faint," the harpy cried and grabbed me. I jerked away and stumbled down the stairs. M caught me. "Whoa, man," he said. "Take it easy. I'll just hang right here with you."

The assembled masses decided I should be x-rayed to make sure I wasn't harboring a fatal wound like a secret grudge with which to accuse them later. As they ushered me toward the ambulance, I heard a familiar voice cry "Hey!" and I looked up. Dad was headed toward us, looking from the ambulance to the mail truck to the bike and to me. He was covered head-to-foot with soot from the furnace, a slightly overdone Pillsbury doughboy.

Dotson paused inside his cloud of cigar smoke and spread his arms, looking up. "Now what?"

"Hey," Dad repeated, gesturing with his glasses toward me in the middle of the crowd. "That's my boy you got there." He looked like Malcom X's brother Y, the short one with the gland problem.

The ambulance driver looked at dark, short, and dumpy Dad and then at M standing next to me, also dark, short, and dumpy. "No, sir, your boy is just fine. It's this one we're taking to x-ray." He took me by the shoulders and lifted me into the front seat of the ambulance. I still held the dishrag in my hand.

"No, no, that's my boy," Dad said, following the ambulance along as it pulled away, looking like an escapee from a minstrel show. I could hear Mrs. Puffy-Screechy wailing, "Oh my goodness, oh my goodness" from her yard.

"It's OK, mister. We're just going to give him an x-ray," the driver said, and rolled up his window. He looked over at me. "Was that your dad?"

I looked back and nodded.

He shrugged, looked out the window, and looked back at me. "Do you want to hear the siren?"

I nodded. And we went to the hospital.

Later that evening I sat in my room under house arrest, charged with unauthorized removal of Heidi's bike from the premises. Heidi was given exclusive custody of my bike until I could earn enough money to repair or replace hers. I was reading *Tom Sawyer.* A dark, round head appeared around the door.

"You conscious, man?"

"Yes, but grounded."

"That's what I figured." M walked in and pulled a flashlight out of his back pocket. We padded lightly up the attic stairs to the secret alcove and sat next to the window, M pointing the flashlight to the ceiling between us. It cast a soft light with heavy shadows around us. "So, what happened at the hospital? Did you have brain surgery?"

"No, just an x-ray."

"Did they find a brain?"

"Ha. Very funny. They said I have a concussion." I had no idea what a concussion was, but it sounded impressive, so I was glad to have one since I had no bandages to show I'd been to the hospital.

"Wow! A concussion! Does it hurt?"

"Not yet. I'll let you know if I feel anything coming on."

"Just think, man, if I hadn't been there, you'd probably be dead right now."

"What?" I hadn't considered this theme and wasn't particularly pleased with its introduction.

"Think about it. What was the difference between you hittin' the side of the truck or being in front of the truck? Maybe a second? A second and a half?"

I replayed the events in my mind. "Yeah, about that."

"Runnin' over me probably slowed you down just enough to make the difference between concussion and coffin."

I didn't say anything. Dust sifted through the beam of the flashlight in front of M's face.

"Do you believe in God?" M asked.

"Of course," I answered automatically.

"All the time?"

"Of course." I looked at M a little closer. "Don't you?"

"Yeah." M looked away and shone the flashlight to the floor, away from his face. The shadows turned upside down. "But not all the time."

"Why not?"

M turned off the flashlight. The alcove plunged into darkness. We sat in silence. Eventually my eyes adjusted to the thin illumination that penetrated the grimy dormer window from the streetlight. M's face was a black moon in a blacker night, eyes lost in shadow.

"Sometimes, there is no God."

I squinted in the dark, trying to see his eyes. He turned his head away from me and his eyes came out of shadow, shining. He looked out of the window into the night. I said nothing.

"Sometimes you pray for somethin', somethin' good, but it never happens. Sometimes you pray for somethin' bad to quit, but it don't."

I said nothing. I rarely bothered God with my problems. Of course I prayed before meals, at least when Mom and Dad were around. And at church. Just the regulation stuff. I had heard of desperate people pleading with God, but I had never done so, probably because I had never been desperate. What did I have to be desperate about? I was only ten years old, for crying out loud!

M kept his gaze riveted to the window. "But today I saved your life. That should count for somethin'." He looked back at me, his eyes veiled in shadow again. "You owe me one. Or maybe God owes me one. Maybe there is some special thing for you to do, and I kept you alive so you can do it."

This whole thing sounded too hypothetical for me. "Or maybe you just happened to be there. Does it have to be some big reason? Maybe it's just for no reason. Maybe it just is."

M sat still for a long time. "You said you believed in God. All the time." With fierce deliberation he breathed, "There is a reason." He switched the light back on and shined it directly in my face. I squinted at him and shielded my eyes with my hand. M turned and walked down the stairs, leaving me in the darkness.

A long time later, I followed.

CHAPTER FIVE

That Christmas something happened that changed my life. I got an AM radio. It was a battery-operated portable, not very big for a milestone, only about the size of a deck of cards. Still, it was an opaque window into another world that didn't have much in common with mine.

Each night, when I was forced to quit reading, I would tune in to WLS AM 890 out of Chicago and put the radio under my pillow. I fell asleep to the world-according-to-pop music in all its eclectic glory—from quirky, weird songs like "Auntie Grezelda" to production masterpieces like "Good Vibrations." I drove my parents crazy by making them turn up the radio whenever Tommy James and the Shondells came on singing "Hanky Panky." Heidi, Hannah, and I sang along without a clue as to what the song was about.

Sometimes strange, disturbing images of another world trickled through in lyrics to songs like "Lucy in the Sky with Diamonds" or "White Rabbit"—images I didn't understand, but were all the more fascinating to me because of their elusiveness.

One weekend we drove down to Kentucky to visit some friends. I was staring out the window as we passed through Cincinnati, looking at all the tall, narrow houses lined up like pastel dominoes waiting for a perverse giant to push the first one. In the downtown traffic we inched past a park. A group of teenagers were hanging around a fountain. They all had long hair, even the guys, and were dressed like they were headed to some kind of psychotic costume party: tie-dyed shirts, hip-hugger bell-bottom jeans, fringed leather vests, headbands, necklaces of various kinds.

"Oh, look," Mom said, pointing out the window.

"Hippies," Dad said, using the same tone of voice he would have used to identify a hippopotamus or giraffe in the zoo.

Hannah giggled. "Hippies!" she repeated.

I was intrigued. "What's a hippie?"

"Young people who live in communes and grow their hair long and wear necklaces they call 'love beads' and take drugs and protest the war," Mom explained. She didn't mention the "free love" thing, which I didn't realize until later, of course.

"That's stupid," Heidi said.

I looked back out the window. "Why are they called hippies?" I expected them to have very large hips.

"I don't know," Mom said.

Dad volunteered some etymology. "It comes from the word hip, which came from the word hep, which means fashionable or knowledgeable about the latest trends."

"Hippies," I whispered to the window as the park faded from view, certain that these hippies were pieces in the puzzle forming from my AM-radio-sponsored lessons in pop culture.

The reference to drugs fascinated me even more. I had heard of acid, heroin, cocaine, and marijuana, of people hearing colors and seeing smells and smelling music. I was very curious about how the senses could trade places, and I wondered what red sounded like. Was it loud? Soothing? Alarming? Obnoxious? Hypnotic? Stories of bad trips and acid flashbacks added a darker, menacing tone to the magical stories. Why did these hippies risk such dangers for the experience? What was I missing that made the reward worth the risks?

From that day forward I listened hungrily to the evening news whenever I saw a protest march or a love-in, grasping for details that would enlighten me about this new world. My tastes in music shifted from pop hits to music with more edge to it. From the Supremes doing "Keep Me Hanging On" to the Vanilla Fudge version, from the Monkees to the Stones.

I also started wondering about the Creature again. I periodically peered through the fence, sometimes catching a glimpse of her brogans jutting out of the box. When it got colder, she disappeared like the robins. One January afternoon I ventured through the gap. The box had collapsed into a soggy ruin. I propped it up. The tattered blanket was still inside, now hardly more than a rag. Nothing else of the Creature remained.

The next Saturday M and I walked to the library, bundled in hats, mufflers, mittens, and overcoats. A low gray blanket shut out the sun. Melted snow left behind a mantle of gray slush that mirrored the sky. The world seemed a muted dreariness. We kicked at the slush with our boots as we trudged along. I told M that I thought the Creature had left.

"Don't even mention her, man," he said with feeling. "It's bad luck to talk about witches."

"She wasn't a witch, just a lady hobo."

"Oh, she wasn't? Didn't you hear her put a curse on me? She tried to turn me into a pig!"

I stopped and looked at M. "What?"

M stopped and turned back. "Yeah, man. She said, 'You will be cursed and become a ham,' or somethin' like that!" He shivered, but not from the cold. "And," he added resentfully, his eyes narrowing into slits, "she said somethin' about me being a slave. I missed some of it when I cleared that fence."

I laughed, puffs of breath floating around my head. M was not amused. He walked on.

I ran to catch up, almost slipping in the slush. "M, she wasn't putting a curse on you; she was quoting the Bible." (Sometimes it comes in handy to be a PK. Not very often though.) "Ham was Noah's third son. After the flood and the ark and two of every animal and the seven of some kinds of animal that nobody ever mentions and the rainbow and all that, Noah got drunk and was lying naked in his tent, and Ham made fun of him, but the other two sons walked into the tent backwards and dropped a robe on him or something, so Noah said that stuff about Ham. Cursed him."

"What?" M stopped, again. "Where did you hear that, man?"

I walked back to him. "It's in the Bible."

"Really? There's stuff like that in the Bible?"

"Oh, yeah. All kinds of stuff like that. Even weirder."

"Really?"

"Really. That's not the half of it."

He considered for awhile, shrugged his shoulders, and we resumed our walk to the library.

"I still think she's a witch," he said.

I pushed him and he slipped on the ice, dragging me down with him. We wrestled in the slush and arrived at the library a little soggier for the trip. I got three Hardy Boys mysteries and *Kidnapped*. M picked up *More Homer Price* and *Sounder.*

On the way back, M introduced a topic that had never come up between us.

"I bet I know who you like." M kicked a can exposed by the melting snow.

I immediately kicked the can back and said, "Who?"

"Pam." He kicked the can back to me.

I faltered and missed the can completely. Every boy had some girl he liked, but it was usually a secret he guarded more jealously than his middle name, assuming, of course, he had an embarrassing middle name, like Maurice. (Apologies to any guys out there named Maurice, but at least your middle name isn't Shirley, like one guy I knew! No apologies to any guys named Shirley.)

I liked M, but he was treading a little too close for my comfort. I hesitated to divulge the truth, but to deny it seemed to betray the girl of my secret affection, and my sense of honor shrank from that dastardly deed. I self-consciously admitted to M that I was entranced by the plain but intelligent Pam.

"And Bingo was his name-o!" M cried just before slipping to the ground in a wail of laughter while attempting a pirouette in the slush.

Of course I wasn't giving this information away for free. After he got back up and picked up all his books, I kicked the can back at him and demanded a corresponding disclosure.

"Guess," he said, with a kick.

I mentally ran through the Negro girls in the class and picked a likely name.

"Nope." Kick.

I picked another.

"Nope." Kick.

I named them all.

"Nope." Kick.

I gave up in exasperation. I figured it must be someone in another grade, and I didn't know many kids in other classes. "So, who is it?" I demanded.

"Terri," he said with a grin.

I was stunned. "Terri?"

"Yeah, Terri."

"Oh." There was no denying Terri was cute, but she was also white. The fact was so glaringly obvious I wondered why M hadn't noticed. I walked in silence for awhile, kicking the can when it came into my lane. Because he was my friend, I felt I should say something. But also, because he was my friend, I didn't want to hurt his feelings. I didn't know how to do both.

"Well . . . I don't . . . I mean, it's not . . . well, I'm not sure that would work out," I said lamely.

"Why not?" he asked.

"Well, because . . . you know." I kept my eyes safely on the can.

There was silence for a moment. "Oh, you mean because—"

"Yeah," I said in a rush, feeling vaguely ashamed without knowing why. We walked on in silence for a long time, the can abandoned behind us in the slush.

We finally arrived on our block. Our library visits had developed into a tradition. The ritual was usually concluded with us repairing to an attic, his or mine as the whim took us, to read for awhile, often with refreshment smuggled up the stairs. This time we stopped on the corner, awkwardly not turning toward either house.

The impasse was broken by M. "You know, Moses' wife was black."

"What?"

"Looks like there's some parts of the Bible you don't know that much about, man."

That decided our destination. A few minutes later we were in Dad's study, still in our coats, steaming slightly on a heater grill, waiting to be noticed. He ceased his labors and peered over large black-frame glasses. "Yes?"

M looked at me. I cleared my throat. "We have a question."

"Yes?"

"About the Bible."

Dad raised one eyebrow, wrinkling the forehead that extended into his scalp. "So, thou hast come to the Oracle. Speak and I shall attend thee." He leaned back in his chair, crossing his hands over his stomach. This little speech didn't phase me. Dad always talked like that. If it had any affect on M, he didn't show it.

I hesitated, a little shy about introducing the topic. I decided there was nothing for it but to plunge forward. "M says that Moses married a Negro woman." I couldn't bring myself to say black even though M had just used it a few minutes ago. It seemed indelicate. My family always used the term Negro. M and I never discussed race, beyond his attempts to educate me about the people he was named after.

Dad nodded his head slowly and looked from me to M and back. "That is certainly one interpretation of Numbers 12."

I raised an eyebrow of my own and stole a glance at M, who was nodding solemnly, vindicated before the authority.

Dad flipped through the Bible on his desk. "The King James Version says, 'And Miriam and Aaron spake against Moses because of the Ethiopian woman whom he had married: for he had married an Ethiopian woman.'" He looked up at me. "Do you remember the Ethiopian missionary who visited our church last year?"

I nodded. The man spoke very strangely, like he hadn't quite mastered the use of his tongue, or like it was slightly too thick for its purpose. He was also the blackest person I had ever seen, much darker than even M, who rarely took second place in the battle of blackness.

"However," Dad continued, "the Revised Standard Version reads a little differently." He pulled another Bible off the shelf behind him. "'Miriam and Aaron spoke against Moses because of the Cushite woman whom he had married, for he had married a Cushite woman.'" He looked up. "Which would mean she was a native of Arabia Chusea, where Saudi Arabia is today. Which would make her race much closer to the Hebrews."

"Does that answer your question?" Dad closed the Bible and returned it to the shelf.

"Yes. Thanks," I said, and we left, climbing to the heights of the attic. M didn't say anything until we were at the top.

"See? What did I tell you?" There was a touch of gloating in his voice.

"Yeah, yeah, so you were right." I sat down and pulled out my book, but didn't open it. I looked out the window for awhile before I spoke again. "I guess the question is, which version does Terri have, King James or Revised Standard?"

M didn't say anything for awhile. He opened a book and held it in his lap, his black thumbs pressed against the white pages. Then, without looking up from the book he was pretending to read, he said, "Yeah, you're probably right."

On a Sunday in March, Heidi received a new bicycle for my eleventh birthday, and my bike was finally restored to its rightful owner. M and I celebrated by riding downtown. We passed the theater, and on a whim I detoured down the alley to perform my periodic check on the Creature's courtyard. When M realized where I was headed, he wasn't happy. I parked my bike and climbed the trash cans. M refused to get off his bike and remained poised to shoot out of the alley at the slightest provocation.

"Relax. She left a long time ago."

"Then why are you checking, man?"

"I don't know. Just habit." I pulled myself over the fence and looked down into the courtyard. The catalog of debris appeared unchanged. God had neither added to its plagues nor taken away from its shares in the tree of life. I was almost back on my bike when I realized that one slight change had indeed occurred. A refrigerator box sat where the washing machine box used to be. I gasped, and M was halfway down the alley before I threw down the bike and returned to the courtyard. I crept to the opening of the box, which faced the gap between the buildings, as before. Inside, a faded red blanket and the familiar stench greeted me. Outside, a few fresh gin bottles were scattered about. The Creature had returned.

Acknowledgments

Thanks to:

- Barry Camp and Mark Wible for inspiring the first incarnation of this work a decade and a half ago
- Rich Bowen for hosting a copy of the original work for the past decade plus, earning him my gratitude and top rankings in Google for the subject
- Daniel Whittington, for providing excellent feedback on early drafts and cover concepts
- Michael Spencer, RIP, who was a great champion of the original work
- Mark Holcomb, who joined me on the journey long ago
- Jeremy Grigg, who provided encouragement and a few good ideas
- Deborah Moss, Darla Hightower, Christianne Squires, and Jevon Bolden, for an eagle eye and a light touch
- Hillary Combs for a fantastic cover
- Jordan Buck for his epub formatting genius
- Tosh McIntosh for his ppub formatting genius and outstanding additional cover design

Extra thanks to those who provided feedback on early drafts:
- Noel Heikkinen, NoelHeikkinen.com
- Dr. Daniel B. Wallace, Center for the Study of New Testament Manuscripts, CSNTM.org
- Daniel Whittington, DanielWhittington.com
- Bill MacKinnon, Boar's Head Tavern Fellow
- Kelly Brewer

Special thanks to those who linked to, referenced, or commented on the original work, including:

- Michael Spencer, InternetMonk.com
- Rich Bowen, DrBacchus.com
- A.J. Jacobs, AJJacobs.com
- Jayson Boyett, JaysonBoyet.com
- Jay Wilson, Brewvana.wordpress.com
- Matt Layton, OnceInAGreatWhile.blogspot.com
- Theological Persiflage, PersiflageThis.blogspot.com
- Dave Armstrong, Socrates58.blogspot.com
- Ken Clark, CreationOutreach.com
- Glen Davis, GlenAndPaula.com
- Andrew Davenport, Tropnevad.org/~adavenpo
- Beth Ley, BLPublications.com
- Chet Day, ChetDay.com
- Michael Schiaparelli, CityBeat.com
- Noel Heikkinen, NoelHeikkinen.com
- Bryon, HomeBrewBeer.net
- Byron Sharp, WineReview.wordpress.com

— BRAD WHITTINGTON —

BradWhittington.com

About the Author

Brad Whittington was born in Fort Worth, Texas, on James Taylor's eighth birthday and Jack Kerouac's thirty-fourth birthday and is old enough to know better. He lives in Austin, Texas, with The Woman. Previously, he has been known to inhabit Hawaii, Ohio, South Carolina, Arizona, and Colorado, annoying people as a janitor, math teacher, field hand, computer programmer, brickyard worker, editor, resident Gentile in a Conservative synagogue, IT director, weed-cutter, and in a number of influential positions in other less notable professions. He is greatly loved and admired by all right-thinking citizens and enjoys a complete absence of cats and dogs at home.

Bibliography

Bacchiocchi, Samuele. *Wine in the Bible: A Biblical Study on the Use of Alcoholic Beverages.* Berrien Springs, MI: Signal Press & Biblical Perspectives, 1989.

Ewing, Charles Wesley. *The Bible and Its Wines.* Denver: National Prohibition Foundation, 1985.

Gentry, Kenneth L. *God Gave Wine: What the Bible Says About Alcohol.* Lincoln, CA: Oakdown Books, 2000.

Libatique, Kelly. *A Toast to the Holy Ghost? A Dispassionate Look at Alcohol and the Bible.* Durham: Eloquent Books, 2010.

Lumpkins, Peter. *Alcohol Today: Abstinence in an Age of Indulgence.* Garland, TX: Hannibal Books, 2009.

Masters, Peter. *Should Christians Drink?: The Case for Total Abstinence.* London: Wakeman Trust, 1992.

Patton, William. *Bible Wines or the Laws of Fermentation and Wines of the Ancients.* New York: National Temperance Society and Publication House, 1891.

Reynolds, Stephen M. and Calel Butler. *The Biblical Approach to Alcohol.* Glenside, PA: Reynolds Foundation, 2003.

Smith, Scott E. *Cracking the Wine Case: Unlocking Ancient Secrets in the Christian and Drinking Controversy.* N.p.: CreateSpace, 2010.

West, Jim. *Drinking With Calvin and Luther: A History of Alcohol in the Church.* Lincoln, CA: Oakdown Books, 2003.

Wilson, J. *Dairy of a Part-Time Monk.* Hampstead, Maryland: Old Line Publishing, 2011.

Appendix: References to Alcohol in the Bible

References to WINE (228)

Abuse (examples of) [1] Citation: GENESIS 009:021

King James: And he drank of the wine, and was drunken; and he was uncovered within his tent.

New International: When he drank some of its wine, he became drunk and lay uncovered inside his tent.

Abuse (examples of) [2] Citation: GENESIS 009:024

King James: And Noah awoke from his wine, and knew what his younger son had done unto him.

New International: When Noah awoke from his wine and found out what his youngest son had done to him,

Use is accepted as normal [3] Citation: GENESIS 014:018

King James: And Melchizedek king of Salem brought forth bread and wine: and he was the priest of the most high God.

New International: Then Melchizedek king of Salem brought out bread and wine. He was priest of God Most High,

Abuse (examples of) [4] Citation: GENESIS 019:032

King James: Come, let us make our father drink wine, and we will lie with him, that we may preserve seed of our father.

New International: Let's get our father to drink wine and then lie with him and preserve our family line through our father.

Abuse (examples of) [5] Citation: GENESIS 019:033

King James: And they made their father drink wine that night: and the firstborn went in, and lay with her father; and he perceived not when she lay down, nor when she arose.

New International: That night they got their father to drink wine, and the older daughter went in and lay with him. He was not aware of it when she lay down or when she got up.

Abuse (examples of) [6] Citation: GENESIS 019:034

King James: And it came to pass on the morrow, that the firstborn said unto the younger, Behold, I lay yesternight with my father: let us make him drink wine this night also; and go thou in, and lie with him, that we may preserve seed of our father.

New International: The next day the older daughter said to the younger, "Last night I lay with my father. Let's get him to drink wine again tonight, and you go in and lie with him so we can preserve our family line through our father."

Abuse (examples of) [7] Citation: GENESIS 019:035

King James: And they made their father drink wine that night also: and the younger arose, and lay with him; and he perceived not when she lay down, nor when she arose.

New International: So they got their father to drink wine that night also, and the younger daughter went and lay with him. Again he was not aware of it when she lay down or when she got up.

Use is accepted as normal [8] Citation: GENESIS 027:025

King James: And he said, Bring it near to me, and I will eat of my son's venison, that my soul may bless thee. And he brought it near to him, and he did eat: and he brought him wine and he drank.

New International: Then he said, "My son, bring me some of your game to eat, so that I may give you my blessing." Jacob brought it to him and he ate; and he brought some wine and he drank.

Blessing from God [9] Citation: GENESIS 027:028

King James: Therefore God give thee of the dew of heaven, and the fatness of the earth, and plenty of corn and wine:

New International: May God give you of heaven's dew and of earth's richness-- an abundance of grain and new wine.

Blessing from God [10] Citation: GENESIS 027:037

King James: And Isaac answered and said unto Esau, Behold, I have made him thy lord, and all his brethren have I given to him for servants; and with corn and wine have I sustained him: and what shall I do now unto thee, my son?

New International: Isaac answered Esau, "I have made him lord over you and have made all his relatives his servants, and I have sustained him with grain and new wine. So what can I possibly do for you, my son?"

Blessing from God [11] Citation: GENESIS 049:011

King James: Binding his foal unto the vine, and his ass's colt unto the choice vine; he washed his garments in wine, and his clothes in the blood of grapes:

New International: He will tether his donkey to a vine, his colt to the choicest branch; he will wash his garments in wine, his robes in the blood of grapes.

Blessing from God [12] Citation: GENESIS 049:012

King James: His eyes shall be red with wine, and his teeth white with milk.

New International: His eyes will be darker than wine, his teeth whiter than milk.

Offering (use in) [13] Citation: EXODUS 029:040

King James: And with the one lamb a tenth deal of flour mingled with the fourth part of an hin of beaten oil; and the fourth part of an hin of wine for a drink offering.

New International: With the first lamb offer a tenth of an ephah of fine flour mixed with a quarter of a hin of oil from pressed olives, and a quarter of a hin of wine as a drink offering.

Vows of abstinence [14] Citation: LEVITICUS 010:009

King James: Do not drink wine nor strong drink, thou, nor thy sons with thee, when ye go into the tabernacle of the congregation, lest ye die: it shall be a statute for ever throughout your generations:

New International: You and your sons are not to drink wine or other fermented drink whenever you go into the Tent of Meeting, or you will die. This is a lasting ordinance for the generations to come.

Offering (use in) [15] Citation: LEVITICUS 023:013

King James: And the meat offering thereof shall be two tenth deals of fine flour mingled with oil, an offering made by fire unto the Lord for a sweet savour: and the drink offering thereof shall be of wine, the fourth part of an hin.

New International: together with its grain offering of two-tenths of an ephah of fine flour mixed with oil--an offering made to the LORD by fire, a pleasing aroma--and its drink offering of a quarter of a hin of wine.

Vows of abstinence [16] Citation: NUMBERS 006:003

King James: He shall separate himself from wine and strong drink, and shall drink no vinegar of wine, or vinegar of strong drink, neither shall he drink any liquor of grapes, nor eat moist grapes, or dried.

New International: he must abstain from wine and other fermented drink and must not drink vinegar made from wine or from other fermented drink. He must not drink grape juice or eat grapes or raisins.

Offering (use in) [17] Citation: NUMBERS 006:020

King James: And the priest shall wave them for a wave offering before the Lord: this is holy for the priest, with the wave breast and heave shoulder: and after that the Nazarite may drink wine.

New International: The priest shall then wave them before the LORD as a wave offering; they are holy and belong to the priest, together with the breast that was waved and the thigh that was presented. After that, the Nazirite may drink wine.

Offering (use in) [18] Citation: NUMBERS 015:005

King James: And the fourth part of an hin of wine for a drink offering shalt thou prepare with the burnt offering or sacrifice, for one lamb.

New International: With each lamb for the burnt offering or the sacrifice, prepare a quarter of a hin of wine as a drink offering.

Offering (use in) [19] Citation: NUMBERS 015:007

King James: And for a drink offering thou shalt offer the third part of an hin of wine, for a sweet savour unto the Lord.

New International: and a third of a hin of wine as a drink offering. Offer it as an aroma pleasing to the LORD.

Offering (use in) [20] Citation: NUMBERS 015:010

King James: And thou shalt bring for a drink offering half an hin of wine, for an offering made by fire, of a sweet savour unto the Lord.

New International: Also bring half a hin of wine as a drink offering. It will be an offering made by fire, an aroma pleasing to the LORD.

Offering (use in) [21] Citation: NUMBERS 018:012

King James: All the best of the oil, and all the best of the wine, and of the wheat, the firstfruits of them which they shall offer unto the Lord, them have I given thee.

New International: "I give you all the finest olive oil and all the finest new wine and grain they give the LORD as the firstfruits of their harvest.

Offering (use in) [22] Citation: NUMBERS 028:007

King James: And the drink offering thereof shall be the fourth part of an hin for the one lamb: in the holy place shalt thou cause the strong wine to be poured unto the Lord for a drink offering.

New International: The accompanying drink offering is to be a quarter of a hin of fermented drink with each lamb. Pour out the drink offering to the LORD at the sanctuary.

Offering (use in) [23] Citation: NUMBERS 028:014

King James: And their drink offerings shall be half an hin of wine unto a bullock, and the third part of an hin unto a ram, and a fourth part of an hin unto a lamb: this is the burnt offering of every month throughout the months of the year.

New International: With each bull there is to be a drink offering of half a hin of wine; with the ram, a third of a hin ; and with each lamb, a quarter of a hin. This is the monthly burnt offering to be made at each new moon during the year.

Blessing from God [24] Citation: DEUTERONOMY 007:013

King James: And he will love thee, and bless thee, and multiply thee: he will also bless the fruit of thy womb, and the fruit of thy land, thy corn, and thy wine, and thine oil, the increase of thy kine, and the flocks of thy sheep, in the land which he sware unto thy fathers to give thee.

New International: He will love you and bless you and increase your numbers. He will bless the fruit of your womb, the crops of your land--your grain, new wine and oil--the calves of your herds and the lambs of your flocks in the land that he swore to your forefathers to give you.

Blessing from God [25] Citation: DEUTERONOMY 011:014

King James: That I will give you the rain of your land in his due season, the first rain and the latter rain, that thou mayest gather in thy corn, and thy wine, and thine oil.

New International: then I will send rain on your land in its season, both autumn and spring rains, so that you may gather in your grain, new wine and oil.

Offering (use in) [26] Citation: DEUTERONOMY 012:017

King James: Thou mayest not eat within thy gates the tithe of thy corn, or of thy wine, or of thy oil, or the firstlings of thy herds or of thy flock, nor any of thy vows which thou vowest, nor thy freewill offerings, or heave offering of thine hand:

New International: You must not eat in your own towns the tithe of your grain and new wine and oil, or the firstborn of your herds and flocks, or whatever you have vowed to give, or your freewill offerings or special gifts.

Offering (use in) [27] Citation: DEUTERONOMY 014:023

King James: And thou shalt eat before the Lord thy God, in the place which he shall choose to place his name there, the tithe of thy corn, of thy wine, and of thine oil, and the firstlings of thy herds and of thy flocks; that thou mayest learn to fear the Lord thy God always.

New International: Eat the tithe of your grain, new wine and oil, and the firstborn of your herds and flocks in the presence of the LORD your God at the place he will choose as a dwelling for his Name, so that you may learn to revere the LORD your God always.

Offering (use in) [28] Citation: DEUTERONOMY 014:026

King James: And thou shalt bestow that money for whatsoever thy soul lusteth after, for oxen, or for sheep, or for wine, or for strong drink, or for whatsoever thy soul desireth: and thou shalt eat there before the Lord thy God, and thou shalt rejoice, thou, and thine household,

New International: Use the silver to buy whatever you like: cattle, sheep, wine or other fermented drink, or anything you wish. Then you and your household shall eat there in the presence of the LORD your God and rejoice.

Use is accepted as normal [29] Citation: DEUTERONOMY 016:013

King James: Thou shalt observe the feast of tabernacles seven days, after that thou hast gathered in thy corn and thy wine:

New International: Celebrate the Feast of Tabernacles for seven days after you have gathered the produce of your threshing floor and your winepress.

Offering (use in) [30] Citation: DEUTERONOMY 018:004

King James: The firstfruit also of thy corn, of thy wine, and of thine oil, and the first of the fleece of thy sheep, shalt thou give him.

New International: You are to give them the firstfruits of your grain, new wine and oil, and the first wool from the shearing of your sheep,

Loss of wine is a curse from God [31] Citation: DEUTERONOMY 028:039

King James: Thou shalt plant vineyards, and dress them, but shalt neither drink of the wine, nor gather the grapes; for the worms shall eat them.

New International: You will plant vineyards and cultivate them but you will not drink the wine or gather the grapes, because worms will eat them.

Loss of wine is a curse from God [32] Citation: DEUTERONOMY 028:051

King James: And he shall eat the fruit of thy cattle, and the fruit of thy land, until thou be destroyed: which also shall not leave thee either corn, wine, or oil, or the increase of thy kine, or flocks of thy sheep, until he have destroyed thee.

New International: They will devour the young of your livestock and the crops of your land until you are destroyed. They will leave you no grain, new wine or oil, nor any calves of your herds or lambs of your flocks until you are ruined.

No specific category [33] Citation: DEUTERONOMY 029:006

King James: Ye have not eaten bread, neither have ye drunk wine or strong drink: that ye might know that I am the Lord your God.

New International: You ate no bread and drank no wine or other fermented drink. I did this so that you might know that I am the LORD your God.

Symbolic [34] Citation: DEUTERONOMY 032:033

King James: Their wine is the poison of dragons, and the cruel venom of asps.

New International: Their wine is the venom of serpents, the deadly poison of cobras.

Offering (use in) [35] Citation: DEUTERONOMY 032:038

King James: Which did eat the fat of their sacrifices, and drank the wine of their drink offerings? let them rise up and help you, and be your protection.

New International: the gods who ate the fat of their sacrifices and drank the wine of their drink offerings? Let them rise up to help you! Let them give you shelter!

Blessing from God [36] Citation: DEUTERONOMY 033:028

King James: Israel then shall dwell in safety alone: the fountain of Jacob shall be upon a land of corn and wine; also his heavens shall drop down dew.

New International: So Israel will live in safety alone; Jacob's spring is secure in a land of grain and new wine, where the heavens drop dew.

Use is accepted as normal [37] Citation: JOSHUA 009:004

King James: They did work wilily, and went and made as if they had been ambassadors, and took old sacks upon their asses, and wine bottles, old, and rent, and bound up;

New International: they resorted to a ruse: They went as a delegation whose donkeys were loaded with worn-out sacks and old wineskins, cracked and mended.

Use is accepted as normal [38] Citation: JOSHUA 009:013

King James: And these bottles of wine, which we filled, were new; and, behold, they be rent: and these our garments and our shoes are become old by reason of the very long journey.

New International: And these wineskins that we filled were new, but see how cracked they are. And our clothes and sandals are worn out by the very long journey."

Blessing from God [39] Citation: JUDGES 009:013

King James: And the vine said unto them, Should I leave my wine, which cheereth God and man, and go to be promoted over the trees?

New International: "But the vine answered, `Should I give up my wine, which cheers both gods and men, to hold sway over the trees?'

Vows of abstinence [40] Citation: JUDGES 013:004

King James: Now therefore beware, I pray thee, and drink not wine nor strong drink, and eat not any unclean thing:

New International: Now see to it that you drink no wine or other fermented drink and that you do not eat anything unclean,

Vows of abstinence [41] Citation: JUDGES 013:007

King James: But he said unto me, Behold, thou shalt conceive, and bear a son; and now drink no wine nor strong drink, neither eat any unclean thing: for the child shall be a Nazarite to God from the womb to the day of his death.

New International: But he said to me, `You will conceive and give birth to a son. Now then, drink no wine or other fermented drink and do not eat anything unclean, because the boy will be a Nazirite of God from birth until the day of his death.'"

Vows of abstinence [42] Citation: JUDGES 013:014

King James: She may not eat of any thing that cometh of the vine, neither let her drink wine or strong drink, nor eat any unclean thing: all that I commanded her let her observe.

New International: She must not eat anything that comes from the grapevine, nor drink any wine or other fermented drink nor eat anything unclean. She must do everything I have commanded her."

Use is accepted as normal [43] Citation: JUDGES 019:019

King James: Yet there is both straw and provender for our asses; and there is bread and wine also for me, and for thy handmaid, and for the young man which is with thy servants: there is no want of any thing.

New International: We have both straw and fodder for our donkeys and bread and wine for ourselves your servants--me, your maidservant, and the young man with us. We don't need anything."

Use is accepted as normal [44] Citation: RUTH 002:014

King James: And Boaz said unto her, At mealtime come thou hither, and eat of the bread, and dip thy morsel in the vinegar. And she sat beside the reapers: and he reached her parched corn, and she did eat, and was sufficed, and left.

New International: At mealtime Boaz said to her, "Come over here. Have some bread and dip it in the wine vinegar." When she sat down with the harvesters, he offered her some roasted grain. She ate all she wanted and had some left over.

False accusations of drunkeness [45] Citation: 1 SAMUEL 001:014

King James: And Eli said unto her, How long wilt thou be drunken? put away thy wine from thee.

New International: and said to her, "How long will you keep on getting drunk? Get rid of your wine."

False accusations of drunkeness [46] Citation: 1 SAMUEL 001:015

King James: And Hannah answered and said, No, my lord, I am a woman of a sorrowful spirit: I have drunk neither wine nor strong drink, but have poured out my soul before the Lord.

New International: "Not so, my lord," Hannah replied, "I am a woman who is deeply troubled. I have not been drinking wine or beer; I was pouring out my soul to the LORD.

Offering (use in) [47] Citation: 1 SAMUEL 001:024

King James: And when she had weaned him, she took him up with her, with three bullocks, and one ephah of flour, and a bottle of wine, and brought him unto the house of the Lord in Shiloh: and the child was young.

New International: After he was weaned, she took the boy with her, young as he was, along with a three-year-old bull, an ephah of flour and a skin of wine, and brought him to the house of the LORD at Shiloh.

Use is accepted as normal [48] Citation: 1 SAMUEL 010:003

King James: Then shalt thou go on forward from thence, and thou shalt come to the plain of Tabor, and there shall meet thee three men going up to God to Bethel, one carrying three kids, and another carrying three loaves of bread, and another carrying a bottle of wine:

New International: "Then you will go on from there until you reach the great tree of Tabor. Three men going up to God at Bethel will meet you there. One will be carrying three young goats, another three loaves of bread, and another a skin of wine.

Gift between people [49] Citation: 1 SAMUEL 016:020

King James: And Jesse took an ass laden with bread, and a bottle of wine, and a kid, and sent them by David his son unto Saul.

New International: So Jesse took a donkey loaded with bread, a skin of wine and a young goat and sent them with his son David to Saul.

Gift between people [50] Citation: 1 SAMUEL 025:018

King James: Then Abigail made haste, and took two hundred loaves, and two bottles of wine, and five sheep ready dressed, and five measures of parched corn, and an hundred clusters of raisins, and two hundred cakes of figs, and laid them on asses.

New International: Abigail lost no time. She took two hundred loaves of bread, two skins of wine, five dressed sheep, five seahs of roasted grain, a hundred cakes of raisins and two hundred cakes of pressed figs, and loaded them on donkeys.

Abuse (examples of) [51] Citation: 1 SAMUEL 025:037

King James: But it came to pass in the morning, when the wine was gone out of Nabal, and his wife had told him these things, that his heart died within him, and he became as a stone.

New International: Then in the morning, when Nabal was sober, his wife told him all these things, and his heart failed him and he became like a stone.

Gift between people [52] Citation: 2 SAMUEL 006:019

King James: And he dealt among all the people, even among the whole multitude of Israel, as well to the women as men, to every one a cake of bread, and a good piece of flesh, and a flagon of wine. So all the people departed every one to his house.

New International: Then he gave a loaf of bread, a cake of dates and a cake of raisins to each person in the whole crowd of Israelites, both men and women. And all the people went to their homes.

No specific category [53] Citation: 2 SAMUEL 013:028

King James: Now Absalom had commanded his servants, saying, Mark ye now when Amnon's heart is merry with wine, and when I say unto you, Smite Amnon; then kill him, fear not: have not I commanded you? be courageous, and be valiant.

New International: Absalom ordered his men, "Listen! When Amnon is in high spirits from drinking wine and I say to you, `Strike Amnon down,' then kill him. Don't be afraid. Have not I given you this order? Be strong and brave."

Gift between people [54] Citation: 2 SAMUEL 016:001

King James: And when David was a little past the top of the hill, behold, Ziba the servant of Mephibosheth met him, with a couple of asses saddled, and upon them two hundred loaves of bread, and an hundred bunches of raisins, and an hundred of summer fruits, and a bottle of wine.

New International: When David had gone a short distance beyond the summit, there was Ziba, the steward of Mephibosheth, waiting to meet him. He had a string of donkeys saddled and loaded with two hundred loaves of bread, a hundred cakes of raisins, a hundred cakes of figs and a skin of wine.

Gift between people [55] Citation: 2 SAMUEL 016:002

King James: And the king said unto Ziba, What meanest thou by these? And Ziba said, The asses be for the king's household to ride on; and the bread and summer fruit for the young men to eat; and the wine, that such as be faint in the wilderness may drink.

New International: The king asked Ziba, "Why have you brought these?" Ziba answered, "The donkeys are for the king's household to ride on, the bread and fruit are for the men to eat, and the wine is to refresh those who become exhausted in the desert."

Use is accepted as normal [56] Citation: 2 KINGS 018:032

King James: Until I come and take you away to a land like your own land, a land of corn and wine, a land of bread and vineyards, a land of oil olive and of honey, that ye may live, and not die: and hearken not unto Hezekiah, when he persuadeth you, saying, The Lord will deliver us.

New International: until I come and take you to a land like your own, a land of grain and new wine, a land of bread and vineyards, a land of olive trees and honey. Choose life and not death! "Do not listen to Hezekiah, for he is misleading you when he says, 'The LORD will deliver us.'

Offering (use in) [57] Citation: 1 CHRONICLES 009:029

King James: Some of them also were appointed to oversee the vessels, and all the instruments of the sanctuary, and the fine flour, and the wine, and the oil, and the frankincense, and the spices.

New International: Others were assigned to take care of the furnishings and all the other articles of the sanctuary, as well as the flour and wine, and the oil, incense and spices.

Gift between people [58] Citation: 1 CHRONICLES 012:040

King James: Moreover they that were nigh them, even unto Issachar and Zebulun and Naphtali, brought bread on asses, and on camels, and on mules, and on oxen, and meat, meal, cakes of figs, and bunches of raisins, and wine, and oil, and oxen, and sheep abundantly: for there was joy in Israel.

New International: Also, their neighbors from as far away as Issachar, Zebulun and Naphtali came bringing food on donkeys, camels, mules and oxen. There were plentiful supplies of flour, fig cakes, raisin cakes, wine, oil, cattle and sheep, for there was joy in Israel.

Gift between people [59] Citation: 1 CHRONICLES 016:003

King James: And he dealt to every one of Israel, both man and woman, to every one a loaf of bread, and a good piece of flesh, and a flagon of wine.

New International: Then he gave a loaf of bread, a cake of dates and a cake of raisins to each Israelite man and woman.

Use is accepted as normal [60] Citation: 1 CHRONICLES 027:027

King James: And over the vineyards was Shimei the Ramathite: over the increase of the vineyards for the wine cellars was Zabdi the Shiphmite:

New International: Shimei the Ramathite was in charge of the vineyards. Zabdi the Shiphmite was in charge of the produce of the vineyards for the wine vats.

Gift between people [61] Citation: 2 CHRONICLES 002:010

King James: And, behold, I will give to thy servants, the hewers that cut timber, twenty thousand measures of beaten wheat, and twenty thousand measures of barley, and twenty thousand baths of wine, and twenty thousand baths of oil.

New International: I will give your servants, the woodsmen who cut the timber, twenty thousand cors of ground wheat, twenty thousand cors of barley, twenty thousand baths of wine and twenty thousand baths of olive oil."

Gift between people [62] Citation: 2 CHRONICLES 002:015

King James: Now therefore the wheat, and the barley, the oil, and the wine, which my lord hath spoken of, let him send unto his servants:

New International: "Now let my lord send his servants the wheat and barley and the olive oil and wine he promised,

Use is accepted as normal [63] Citation: 2 CHRONICLES 011:011

King James: And he fortified the strong holds, and put captains in them, and store of victual, and of oil and wine.

New International: He strengthened their defenses and put commanders in them, with supplies of food, olive oil and wine.

Offering (use in) [64] Citation: 2 CHRONICLES 031:005

King James: And as soon as the commandment came abroad, the

children of Israel brought in abundance the firstfruits of corn, wine, and oil, and honey, and of all the increase of the field; and the tithe of all things brought they in abundantly.

New International: As soon as the order went out, the Israelites generously gave the firstfruits of their grain, new wine, oil and honey and all that the fields produced. They brought a great amount, a tithe of everything.

Blessing from God [65] Citation: 2 CHRONICLES 032:028

King James: Storehouses also for the increase of corn, and wine, and oil; and stalls for all manner of beasts, and cotes for flocks.

New International: He also made buildings to store the harvest of grain, new wine and oil; and he made stalls for various kinds of cattle, and pens for the flocks.

Offering (use in) [66] Citation: EZRA 006:009

King James: And that which they have need of, both young bullocks, and rams, and lambs, for the burnt offerings of the God of heaven, wheat, salt, wine, and oil, according to the appointment of the priests which are at Jerusalem, let it be given them day by day without fail:

New International: Whatever is needed--young bulls, rams, male lambs for burnt offerings to the God of heaven, and wheat, salt, wine and oil, as requested by the priests in Jerusalem--must be given them daily without fail,

Use is accepted as normal [67] Citation: EZRA 007:022

King James: Unto an hundred talents of silver, and to an hundred measures of wheat, and to an hundred baths of wine, and to an hundred baths of oil, and salt without prescribing how much.

New International: up to a hundred talents of silver, a hundred cors of wheat, a hundred baths of wine, a hundred baths of olive oil, and salt without limit.

Use is accepted as normal [68] Citation: NEHEMIAH 002:001

King James: And it came to pass in the month Nisan, in the twentieth year of Artaxerxes the king, that wine was before him: and I took up the wine, and gave it unto the king. Now I had not been beforetime sad in his presence.

New International: In the month of Nisan in the twentieth year of King Artaxerxes, when wine was brought for him, I took the wine and gave it to the king. I had not been sad in his presence before;

Use is accepted as normal [69] Citation: NEHEMIAH 005:011

King James: Restore, I pray you, to them, even this day, their lands, their vineyards, their oliveyards, and their houses, also the hundredth part of the money, and of the corn, the wine, and the oil, that ye exact of them.

New International: Give back to them immediately their fields, vineyards, olive groves and houses, and also the usury you are charging them--the hundredth part of the money, grain, new wine and oil."

Use is accepted as normal [70] Citation: NEHEMIAH 005:015

King James: But the former governors that had been before me were chargeable unto the people, and had taken of them bread and wine, beside forty shekels of silver; yea, even their servants bare rule over the people: but so did not I, because of the fear of God.

New International: But the earlier governors--those preceding me--placed a heavy burden on the people and took forty shekels of silver from them in addition to food and wine. Their assistants also lorded it over the people. But out of reverence for God I did not act like that.

Use is accepted as normal [71] Citation: NEHEMIAH 005:018

King James: Now that which was prepared for me daily was one ox and six choice sheep; also fowls were prepared for me, and once in ten days store of all sorts of wine: yet for all this required not I the bread of the governor, because the bondage was heavy upon this people.

New International: Each day one ox, six choice sheep and some poultry were prepared for me, and every ten days an abundant supply of wine of all kinds. In spite of all this, I never demanded the food allotted to the governor, because the demands were heavy on these people.

Offering (use in) [72] Citation: NEHEMIAH 010:037

King James: And that we should bring the firstfruits of our dough, and our offerings, and the fruit of all manner of trees, of wine and of oil, unto the priests, to the chambers of the house of our God; and the tithes of our ground unto the Levites, that the same Levites might have the tithes in all the cities of our tillage.

New International: "Moreover, we will bring to the storerooms of the house of our God, to the priests, the first of our ground meal, of our [grain] offerings, of the fruit of all our trees and of our new wine and oil. And we will bring a tithe of our crops to the Levites, for it is the Levites who collect the tithes in all the towns where we work.

Offering (use in) [73] Citation: NEHEMIAH 010:039

King James: For the children of Israel and the children of Levi shall bring the offering of the corn, of the new wine, and the oil, unto the chambers, where are the vessels of the sanctuary, and priests that minister, and the porters, and the singers: and we will not forsake the house of our God.

New International: The people of Israel, including the Levites, are to bring their contributions of grain, new wine and oil to the storerooms where the articles for the sanctuary are kept and where the ministering priests, the gatekeepers and the singers stay. "We will not neglect the house of our God."

Offering (use in) [74] Citation: NEHEMIAH 013:005

King James: And he had prepared for him a great chamber, where aforetime they laid the meat offerings, the frankincense, and the vessels, and the tithes of the corn, the new wine, and the oil, which was commanded to be given to the Levites, and the singers, and the porters; and the offerings of the priests.

New International: and he had provided him with a large room formerly used to store the grain offerings and incense and temple articles, and also the tithes of grain, new wine and oil prescribed for the Levites, singers and gatekeepers, as well as the contributions for the priests.

Offering (use in) [75] Citation: NEHEMIAH 013:012

King James: Then brought all Judah the tithe of the corn and the new wine and the oil unto the treasuries.

New International: All Judah brought the tithes of grain, new wine and oil into the storerooms.

Offering (use in) [76] Citation: NEHEMIAH 013:015

King James: In those days saw I in Judah some treading wine presses on the sabbath, and bringing in sheaves, and lading asses; as also wine, grapes, and figs, and all manner of burdens, which they brought into Jerusalem on the sabbath day: and I testified against them in the day wherein they sold victuals.

New International: In those days I saw men in Judah treading winepresses on the Sabbath and bringing in grain and loading it on donkeys, together with wine, grapes, figs and all other kinds of loads. And they were bringing all this into Jerusalem on the Sabbath. Therefore I warned them against selling food on that day.

Use is accepted as normal [77] Citation: ESTHER 001:007

King James: And they gave them drink in vessels of gold, (the vessels being diverse one from another,) and royal wine in abundance, according to the state of the king.

New International: Wine was served in goblets of gold, each one different from the other, and the royal wine was abundant, in keeping with the king's liberality.

Use is accepted as normal [78] Citation: ESTHER 001:008

King James: And the drinking was according to the law; none did compel: for so the king had appointed to all the officers of his house, that they should do according to every man's pleasure.

New International: By the king's command each guest was allowed to drink in his own way, for the king instructed all the wine stewards to serve each man what he wished.

Use is accepted as normal [79] Citation: ESTHER 001:010

King James: On the seventh day, when the heart of the king was merry with wine, he commanded Mehuman, Biztha, Harbona, Bigtha, and Abagtha, Zethar, and Carcas, the seven chamberlains that served in the presence of Ahasuerus the king,

New International: On the seventh day, when King Xerxes was in high spirits from wine, he commanded the seven eunuchs who served him--Mehuman, Biztha, Harbona, Bigtha, Abagtha, Zethar and Carcas--

Use is accepted as normal [80] Citation: ESTHER 005:006

King James: And the king said unto Esther at the banquet of wine, What is thy petition? and it shall be granted thee: and what is thy request? even to the half of the kingdom it shall be performed.

New International: As they were drinking wine, the king again asked Esther, "Now what is your petition? It will be given you. And what is your request? Even up to half the kingdom, it will be granted."

Use is accepted as normal [81] Citation: ESTHER 007:002

King James: And the king said again unto Esther on the second day at the banquet of wine, What is thy petition, queen Esther? and it shall be granted thee: and what is thy request? and it shall be performed, even to the half of the kingdom.

New International: and as they were drinking wine on that second day, the king again asked, "Queen Esther, what is your petition? It will be given you. What is your request? Even up to half the kingdom, it will be granted."

Use is accepted as normal [82] Citation: ESTHER 007:007

King James: And the king arising from the banquet of wine in his wrath went into the palace garden: and Haman stood up to make request for his life to Esther the queen; for he saw that there was evil determined against him by the king.

New International: The king got up in a rage, left his wine and went out into the palace garden. But Haman, realizing that the king had already decided his fate, stayed behind to beg Queen Esther for his life.

Use is accepted as normal [83] Citation: ESTHER 007:008

King James: Then the king returned out of the palace garden into the place of the banquet of wine; and Haman was fallen upon the bed whereon Esther was. Then said the king, Will he force the queen also before me in the house? As the word went out of the king's mouth, they covered Haman's face.

New International: Just as the king returned from the palace garden to the banquet hall, Haman was falling on the couch where Esther was reclining. The king exclaimed, "Will he even molest the queen while she is with me in the house?" As soon as the word left the king's mouth, they covered Haman's face.

Use is accepted as normal [84] Citation: JOB 001:013

King James: And there was a day when his sons and his daughters were eating and drinking wine in their eldest brother's house:

New International: One day when Job's sons and daughters were feasting and drinking wine at the oldest brother's house,

Use is accepted as normal [85] Citation: JOB 001:018

King James: While he was yet speaking, there came also another, and said, Thy sons and thy daughters were eating and drinking wine in their eldest brother's house:

New International: While he was still speaking, yet another messenger came and said, "Your sons and daughters were feasting and drinking wine at the oldest brother's house,

Symbolic [86] Citation: JOB 032:019

King James: Behold, my belly is as wine which hath no vent; it is ready to burst like new bottles.

New International: inside I am like bottled-up wine, like new wineskins ready to burst.

Blessing from God [87] Citation: PSALMS 004:007

King James: Thou hast put gladness in my heart, more than in the time that their corn and their wine increased.

New International: You have filled my heart with greater joy than when their grain and new wine abound.

Symbolic [88] Citation: PSALMS 060:003

King James: Thou hast shewed thy people hard things: thou hast made us to drink the wine of astonishment.

New International: You have shown your people desperate times; you have given us wine that makes us stagger.

Symbolic [89] Citation: PSALMS 075:008

King James: For in the hand of the Lord there is a cup, and the wine is red; it is full of mixture; and he poureth out of the same: but the dregs thereof, all the wicked of the earth shall wring them out, and drink them.

New International: In the hand of the LORD is a cup full of foaming wine mixed with spices; he pours it out, and all the wicked of the earth drink it down to its very dregs.

Symbolic [90] Citation: PSALMS 078:065

King James: Then the Lord awaked as one out of sleep, and like a mighty man that shouteth by reason of wine.

New International: Then the Lord awoke as from sleep, as a man wakes from the stupor of wine.

Blessing from God [91] Citation: PSALMS 104:015

King James: And wine that maketh glad the heart of man, and oil to make his face to shine, and bread which strengtheneth man's heart.

New International: wine that gladdens the heart of man, oil to make his face shine, and bread that sustains his heart.

Blessing from God [92] Citation: PROVERBS 003:010

King James: So shall thy barns be filled with plenty, and thy presses shall burst out with new wine.

New International: then your barns will be filled to overflowing, and your vats will brim over with new wine.

Symbolic [93] Citation: PROVERBS 004:017

King James: For they eat the bread of wickedness, and drink the wine of violence.

New International: They eat the bread of wickedness and drink the wine of violence.

Use is accepted as normal [94] Citation: PROVERBS 009:002

King James: She hath killed her beasts; she hath mingled her wine; she hath also furnished her table.

New International: She has prepared her meat and mixed her wine; she has also set her table.

Use is accepted as normal [95] Citation: PROVERBS 009:005

King James: Come, eat of my bread, and drink of the wine which I have mingled.

New International: "Come, eat my food and drink the wine I have mixed.

Warnings against abuse [96] Citation: PROVERBS 020:001

King James: Wine is a mocker, strong drink is raging: and whosoever is deceived thereby is not wise.

New International: Wine is a mocker and beer a brawler; whoever is led astray by them is not wise.

Warnings against abuse [97] Citation: PROVERBS 021:017

King James: He that loveth pleasure shall be a poor man: he that loveth wine and oil shall not be rich.

New International: He who loves pleasure will become poor; whoever loves wine and oil will never be rich.

Warnings against abuse [98] Citation: PROVERBS 023:020

King James: Be not among winebibbers; among riotous eaters of flesh:

New International: Do not join those who drink too much wine or gorge themselves on meat,

Warnings against abuse [99] Citation: PROVERBS 023:030

King James: They that tarry long at the wine; they that go to seek mixed wine.

New International: Those who linger over wine, who go to sample bowls of mixed wine.

Warnings against abuse [100] Citation: PROVERBS 023:031

King James: Look not thou upon the wine when it is red, when it giveth his colour in the cup, when it moveth itself aright.

New International: Do not gaze at wine when it is red, when it sparkles in the cup, when it goes down smoothly!

Warnings against abuse [101] Citation: PROVERBS 031:004

King James: It is not for kings, O Lemuel, it is not for kings to drink wine; nor for princes strong drink:

New International: "It is not for kings, O Lemuel-- not for kings to drink wine, not for rulers to crave beer,

Use is accepted as normal [102] Citation: PROVERBS 031:006

King James: Give strong drink unto him that is ready to perish, and wine unto those that be of heavy hearts.

New International: Give beer to those who are perishing, wine to those who are in anguish;

Use is accepted as normal [103] Citation: ECCLESIASTES 002:003

King James: I sought in mine heart to give myself unto wine, yet acquainting mine heart with wisdom; and to lay hold on folly, till I might see what was that good for the sons of men, which they should do under the heaven all the days of their life.

New International: I tried cheering myself with wine, and embracing folly--my mind still guiding me with wisdom. I wanted to see what was worthwhile for men to do under heaven during the few days of their lives.

Blessing from God [104] Citation: ECCLESIASTES 009:007

King James: Go thy way, eat thy bread with joy, and drink thy wine with a merry heart; for God now accepteth thy works.

New International: Go, eat your food with gladness, and drink your wine with a joyful heart, for it is now that God favors what you do.

Blessing from God [105] Citation: ECCLESIASTES 010:019

King James: A feast is made for laughter, and wine maketh merry: but money answereth all things.

New International: A feast is made for laughter, and wine makes life merry, but money is the answer for everything.

Comparison (x is better than wine) [106] Citation: SONG OF SOLOMON 001:002

King James: Let him kiss me with the kisses of his mouth: for thy love is better than wine.

New International: Let him kiss me with the kisses of his mouth-- for your love is more delightful than wine.

Comparison (x is better than wine) [107] Citation: SONG OF SOLOMON 001:004

King James: Draw me, we will run after thee: the king hath brought me into his chambers: we will be glad and rejoice in thee, we will remember thy love more than wine: the upright love thee.

New International: Take me away with you--let us hurry! Let the king bring me into his chambers. We rejoice and delight in you ; we will praise your love more than wine. How right they are to adore you!

Comparison (x is better than wine) [108] Citation: SONG OF SOLOMON 004:010

King James: How fair is thy love, my sister, my spouse! how much better is thy love than wine! and the smell of thine ointments than all spices!

New International: How delightful is your love, my sister, my bride! How much more pleasing is your love than wine, and the fragrance of your perfume than any spice!

Use is accepted as normal [109] Citation: SONG OF SOLOMON 005:001

King James: I am come into my garden, my sister, my spouse: I have gathered my myrrh with my spice; I have eaten my honeycomb with my honey; I have drunk my wine with my milk: eat, O friends; drink, yea, drink abundantly, O beloved.

New International: I have come into my garden, my sister, my bride; I have gathered my myrrh with my spice. I have eaten my honeycomb and my honey; I have drunk my wine and my milk. Eat, O friends, and drink; drink your fill, O lovers.

Comparison (x is better than wine) [110] Citation: SONG OF SOLOMON 007:002

King James: Thy navel is like a round goblet, which wanteth not liquor: thy belly is like an heap of wheat set about with lilies.

New International: Your navel is a rounded goblet that never lacks blended wine. Your waist is a mound of wheat encircled by lilies.

Comparison (x is better than wine) [111] Citation: SONG OF SOLOMON 007:009

King James: And the roof of thy mouth like the best wine for my beloved, that goeth down sweetly, causing the lips of those that are asleep to speak.

New International: and your mouth like the best wine. May the wine go straight to my lover, flowing gently over lips and teeth.

Use is accepted as normal [112] Citation: SONG OF SOLOMON 008:002

King James: I would lead thee, and bring thee into my mother's house, who would instruct me: I would cause thee to drink of spiced wine of the juice of my pomegranate.

New International: I would lead you and bring you to my mother's house-- she who has taught me. I would give you spiced wine to drink, the nectar of my pomegranates.

Loss of wine is a curse from God [113] Citation: ISAIAH 001:022

King James: Thy silver is become dross, thy wine mixed with water:

New International: Your silver has become dross, your choice wine is diluted with water.

Loss of wine is a curse from God [114] Citation: ISAIAH 005:010

King James: Yea, ten acres of vineyard shall yield one bath, and the seed of an homer shall yield an ephah.

New International: A ten-acre vineyard will produce only a bath of wine, a homer of seed only an ephah of grain."

Warnings against abuse [115] Citation: ISAIAH 005:011

King James: Woe unto them that rise up early in the morning, that they may follow strong drink; that continue until night, till wine inflame them!

New International: Woe to those who rise early in the morning to run after their drinks, who stay up late at night till they are inflamed with wine.

Warnings against abuse [116] Citation: ISAIAH 005:012

King James: And the harp, and the viol, the tabret, and pipe, and wine, are in their feasts: but they regard not the work of the Lord, neither consider the operation of his hands.

New International: They have harps and lyres at their banquets, tambourines and flutes and wine, but they have no regard for the deeds of the LORD, no respect for the work of his hands.

Warnings against abuse [117] Citation: ISAIAH 005:022

King James: Woe unto them that are mighty to drink wine, and men of strength to mingle strong drink:

New International: Woe to those who are heroes at drinking wine and champions at mixing drinks,

Loss of wine is a curse from God [118] Citation: ISAIAH 016:010

King James: And gladness is taken away, and joy out of the plentiful field; and in the vineyards there shall be no singing, neither shall there be shouting: the treaders shall tread out no wine in their presses; I have made their vintage shouting to cease.

New International: Joy and gladness are taken away from the orchards; no one sings or shouts in the vineyards; no one treads out wine at the presses, for I have put an end to the shouting.

No specific category [119] Citation: ISAIAH 022:013

King James: And behold joy and gladness, slaying oxen, and killing sheep, eating flesh, and drinking wine: let us eat and drink; for to morrow we shall die.

New International: But see, there is joy and revelry, slaughtering of cattle and killing of sheep, eating of meat and drinking of wine! "Let us eat and drink," you say, "for tomorrow we die!"

Loss of wine is a curse from God [120] Citation: ISAIAH 024:007

King James: The new wine mourneth, the vine languisheth, all the merryhearted do sigh.

New International: The new wine dries up and the vine withers; all the merrymakers groan.

Loss of wine is a curse from God [121] Citation: ISAIAH 024:009

King James: They shall not drink wine with a song; strong drink shall be bitter to them that drink it.

New International: No longer do they drink wine with a song; the beer is bitter to its drinkers.

Loss of wine is a curse from God [122] Citation: ISAIAH 024:011

King James: There is a crying for wine in the streets; all joy is darkened, the mirth of the land is gone.

New International: In the streets they cry out for wine; all joy turns to gloom, all gaiety is banished from the earth.

Blessing from God [123] Citation: ISAIAH 025:006

King James: And in this mountain shall the Lord of hosts make unto all people a feast of fat things, a feast of wines on the lees, of fat things full of marrow, of wines on the lees well refined.

New International: On this mountain the LORD Almighty will prepare a feast of rich food for all peoples, a banquet of aged wine-- the best of meats and the finest of wines.

Blessing from God [124] Citation: ISAIAH 027:002

King James: In that day sing ye unto her, A vineyard of red wine.

New International: In that day-- "Sing about a fruitful vineyard:

Warnings against abuse [125] Citation: ISAIAH 028:001

King James: Woe to the crown of pride, to the drunkards of Ephraim, whose glorious beauty is a fading flower, which are on the head of the fat valleys of them that are overcome with wine!

New International: Woe to that wreath, the pride of Ephraim's drunkards, to the fading flower, his glorious beauty, set on the head of a fertile valley-- to that city, the pride of those laid low by wine!

Abuse (examples of) [126] Citation: ISAIAH 028:007

King James: But they also have erred through wine, and through strong drink are out of the way; the priest and the prophet have erred through strong drink, they are swallowed up of wine, they are out of the way through strong drink; they err in vision, they stumble in judgment.

New International: And these also stagger from wine and reel from beer: Priests and prophets stagger from beer and are befuddled with wine; they reel from beer, they stagger when seeing visions, they stumble when rendering decisions.

Symbolic [127] Citation: ISAIAH 029:009

King James: Stay yourselves, and wonder; cry ye out, and cry: they are drunken, but not with wine; they stagger, but not with strong drink.

New International: Be stunned and amazed, blind yourselves and be sightless; be drunk, but not from wine, stagger, but not from beer.

Use is accepted as normal [128] Citation: ISAIAH 036:017

King James: Until I come and take you away to a land like your own land, a land of corn and wine, a land of bread and vineyards.

New International: until I come and take you to a land like your own--a land of grain and new wine, a land of bread and vineyards.

Symbolic [129] Citation: ISAIAH 049:026

King James: And I will feed them that oppress thee with their own flesh; and they shall be drunken with their own blood, as with sweet wine: and all flesh shall know that I the Lord am thy Saviour and thy Redeemer, the mighty One of Jacob.

New International: I will make your oppressors eat their own flesh; they will be drunk on their own blood, as with wine. Then all mankind will know that I, the LORD, am your Savior, your Redeemer, the Mighty One of Jacob."

Symbolic [130] Citation: ISAIAH 051:021

King James: Therefore hear now this, thou afflicted, and drunken, but not with wine:

New International: Therefore hear this, you afflicted one, made drunk, but not with wine.

Blessing from God [131] Citation: ISAIAH 055:001

King James: Ho, every one that thirsteth, come ye to the waters, and he that hath no money; come ye, buy, and eat; yea, come, buy wine and milk without money and without price.

New International: "Come, all you who are thirsty, come to the waters; and you who have no money, come, buy and eat! Come, buy wine and milk without money and without cost.

Abuse (examples of) [132] Citation: ISAIAH 056:012

King James: Come ye, say they, I will fetch wine, and we will fill ourselves with strong drink; and to morrow shall be as this day, and much more abundant.

New International: "Come," each one cries, "let me get wine! Let us drink our fill of beer! And tomorrow will be like today, or even far better."

Loss of wine is a curse from God [133] Citation: ISAIAH 062:008

King James: The Lord hath sworn by his right hand, and by the arm of his strength, Surely I will no more give thy corn to be meat for thine enemies; and the sons of the stranger shall not drink thy wine, for the which thou hast laboured:

New International: The LORD has sworn by his right hand and by his mighty arm: "Never again will I give your grain as food for your enemies, and never again will foreigners drink the new wine for which you have toiled;

Symbolic [134] Citation: ISAIAH 065:008

King James: Thus saith the Lord, As the new wine is found in the cluster, and one saith, Destroy it not; for a blessing is in it: so will I do for my servants' sakes, that I may not destroy them all.

New International: This is what the LORD says: "As when juice is still found in a cluster of grapes and men say, 'Don't destroy it, there is yet some good in it,' so will I do in behalf of my servants; I will not destroy them all.

Symbolic [135] Citation: ISAIAH 065:011

King James: But ye are they that forsake the Lord, that forget my holy mountain, that prepare a table for that troop, and that furnish the drink offering unto that number.

New International: "But as for you who forsake the LORD and forget my holy mountain, who spread a table for Fortune and fill bowls of mixed wine for Destiny,

Symbolic [136] Citation: JEREMIAH 013:012

King James: Therefore thou shalt speak unto them this word; Thus saith the Lord God of Israel, Every bottle shall be filled with wine: and they shall say unto thee, Do we not certainly know that every bottle shall be filled with wine?

New International: "Say to them: `This is what the LORD, the God of Israel, says: Every wineskin should be filled with wine.' And if they say to you, `Don't we know that every wineskin should be filled with wine?'

Symbolic [137] Citation: JEREMIAH 023:009

King James: Mine heart within me is broken because of the prophets; all my bones shake; I am like a drunken man, and like a man whom wine hath overcome, because of the Lord, and because of the words of his holiness.

New International: Concerning the prophets: My heart is broken within me; all my bones tremble. I am like a drunken man, like a man overcome by wine, because of the LORD and his holy words.

Symbolic [138] Citation: JEREMIAH 025:015

King James: For thus saith the Lord God of Israel unto me; Take the wine cup of this fury at my hand, and cause all the nations, to whom I send thee, to drink it.

New International: This is what the LORD, the God of Israel, said to me: "Take from my hand this cup filled with the wine of my wrath and make all the nations to whom I send you drink it.

Blessing from God [139] Citation: JEREMIAH 031:012

King James: Therefore they shall come and sing in the height of Zion, and shall flow together to the goodness of the Lord, for wheat, and for wine, and for oil, and for the young of the flock and of the herd: and their soul shall be as a watered garden; and they shall not sorrow any more at all.

New International: They will come and shout for joy on the heights of Zion; they will rejoice in the bounty of the LORD-- the grain, the new wine and the oil, the young of the flocks and herds. They will be like a well-watered garden, and they will sorrow no more.

Use is accepted as normal [140] Citation: JEREMIAH 035:002

King James: Go unto the house of the Rechabites, and speak unto them, and bring them into the house of the Lord, into one of the chambers, and give them wine to drink.

New International: "Go to the Recabite family and invite them to come to one of the side rooms of the house of the LORD and give them wine to drink."

Use is accepted as normal [141] Citation: JEREMIAH 035:005

King James: And I set before the sons of the house of the Rechabites pots full of wine, and cups, and I said unto them, Drink ye wine.

New International: Then I set bowls full of wine and some cups before the men of the Recabite family and said to them, "Drink some wine."

Vows of abstinence [142] Citation: JEREMIAH 035:006

King James: But they said, We will drink no wine: for Jonadab the son of Rechab our father commanded us, saying, Ye shall drink no wine, neither ye, nor your sons for ever:

New International: But they replied, "We do not drink wine, because our forefather Jonadab son of Recab gave us this command: `Neither you nor your descendants must ever drink wine.

Vows of abstinence [143] Citation: JEREMIAH 035:008

King James: Thus have we obeyed the voice of Jonadab the son of Rechab our father in all that he hath charged us, to drink no wine all our days, we, our wives, our sons, nor our daughters;

New International: We have obeyed everything our forefather Jonadab son of Recab commanded us. Neither we nor our wives nor our sons and daughters have ever drunk wine

Vows of abstinence [144] Citation: JEREMIAH 035:014

King James: The words of Jonadab the son of Rechab, that he commanded his sons not to drink wine, are performed; for unto this day they drink none, but obey their father's commandment: notwithstanding I have spoken unto you, rising early and speaking; but ye hearkened not unto me.

New International: 'Jonadab son of Recab ordered his sons not to drink wine and this command has been kept. To this day they do not drink wine, because they obey their forefather's command. But I have spoken to you again and again, yet you have not obeyed me.

Use is accepted as normal [145] Citation: JEREMIAH 040:010

King James: As for me, behold, I will dwell at Mizpah, to serve the Chaldeans, which will come unto us: but ye, gather ye wine, and summer fruits, and oil, and put them in your vessels, and dwell in your cities that ye have taken.

New International: I myself will stay at Mizpah to represent you before the Babylonians who come to us, but you are to harvest the wine, summer fruit and oil, and put them in your storage jars, and live in the towns you have taken over."

Use is accepted as normal [146] Citation: JEREMIAH 040:012

King James: Even all the Jews returned out of all places whither they were driven, and came to the land of Judah, to Gedaliah, unto Mizpah, and gathered wine and summer fruits very much.

New International: they all came back to the land of Judah, to Gedaliah at Mizpah, from all the countries where they had been scattered. And they harvested an abundance of wine and summer fruit.

Symbolic [147] Citation: JEREMIAH 048:011

King James: Moab hath been at ease from his youth, and he hath settled on his lees, and hath not been emptied from vessel to vessel, neither hath he gone into captivity: therefore his taste remained in him, and his scent is not changed.

New International: "Moab has been at rest from youth, like wine left on its dregs, not poured from one jar to another-- she has not gone into exile. So she tastes as she did, and her aroma is unchanged.

Loss of wine is a curse from God [148] Citation: JEREMIAH 048:033

King James: And joy and gladness is taken from the plentiful field, and from the land of Moab, and I have caused wine to fail from the winepresses: none shall tread with shouting; their shouting shall be no shouting.

New International: Joy and gladness are gone from the orchards and fields of Moab. I have stopped the flow of wine from the presses; no one treads them with shouts of joy. Although there are shouts, they are not shouts of joy.

Symbolic [149] Citation: JEREMIAH 051:007

King James: Babylon hath been a golden cup in the Lord's hand, that made all the earth drunken: the nations have drunken of her wine; therefore the nations are mad.

New International: Babylon was a gold cup in the LORD's hand; she made the whole earth drunk. The nations drank her wine; therefore they have now gone mad.

Loss of wine is a curse from God [150] Citation: LAMENTATIONS 002:012

King James: They say to their mothers, Where is corn and wine? when they swooned as the wounded in the streets of the city, when their soul was poured out into their mothers' bosom.

New International: They say to their mothers, ÒWhere is bread and wine?Ó as they faint like the wounded in the streets of the city, as their lives ebb away in their mothersÕ arms.

Use is accepted as normal [151] Citation: EZEKIEL 027:018

King James: Damascus was thy merchant in the multitude of the wares of thy making, for the multitude of all riches; in the wine of

Helbon, and white wool.

New International: "`Damascus, because of your many products and great wealth of goods, did business with you in wine from Helbon and wool from Zahar.

Vows of abstinence [152] Citation: EZEKIEL 044:021

King James: Neither shall any priest drink wine, when they enter into the inner court.

New International: No priest is to drink wine when he enters the inner court.

Use is accepted as normal [153] Citation: DANIEL 001:005

King James: And the king appointed them a daily provision of the king's meat, and of the wine which he drank: so nourishing them three years, that at the end thereof they might stand before the king.

New International: The king assigned them a daily amount of food and wine from the king's table. They were to be trained for three years, and after that they were to enter the king's service.

Vows of abstinence [154] Citation: DANIEL 001:008

King James: But Daniel purposed in his heart that he would not defile himself with the portion of the king's meat, nor with the wine which he drank: therefore he requested of the prince of the eunuchs that he might not defile himself.

New International: But Daniel resolved not to defile himself with the royal food and wine, and he asked the chief official for permission not to defile himself this way.

Use is accepted as normal [155] Citation: DANIEL 001:016

King James: Thus Melzar took away the portion of their meat, and the wine that they should drink; and gave them pulse.

New International: So the guard took away their choice food and the wine they were to drink and gave them vegetables instead.

Use is accepted as normal [156] Citation: DANIEL 005:001

King James: Belshazzar the king made a great feast to a thousand of his lords, and drank wine before the thousand.

New International: King Belshazzar gave a great banquet for a thousand of his nobles and drank wine with them.

Use is accepted as normal [157] Citation: DANIEL 005:002

King James: Belshazzar, whiles he tasted the wine, commanded to bring the golden and silver vessels which his father Nebuchadnezzar had taken out of the temple which was in Jerusalem; that the king, and his princes, his wives, and his concubines, might drink therein.

New International: While Belshazzar was drinking his wine, he gave orders to bring in the gold and silver goblets that Nebuchadnezzar his father had taken from the temple in Jerusalem, so that the king and his nobles, his wives and his concubines might drink from them.

Use is accepted as normal [158] Citation: DANIEL 005:004

King James: They drank wine, and praised the gods of gold, and of silver, of brass, of iron, of wood, and of stone.

New International: As they drank the wine, they praised the gods of gold and silver, of bronze, iron, wood and stone.

Use is accepted as normal [159] Citation: DANIEL 005:023

King James: But hast lifted up thyself against the Lord of heaven; and they have brought the vessels of his house before thee, and thou, and thy lords, thy wives, and thy concubines, have drunk wine in them; and thou hast praised the gods of silver, and gold, of brass, iron, wood, and stone, which see not, nor hear, nor know: and the God in whose hand thy breath is, and whose are all thy ways, hast thou not glorified:

New International: Instead, you have set yourself up against the Lord of heaven. You had the goblets from his temple brought to you, and you and your nobles, your wives and your concubines drank wine from them. You praised the gods of silver and gold, of bronze, iron, wood and stone, which cannot see or hear or understand. But you did not honor the God who holds in his hand your life and all your ways.

Vows of abstinence [160] Citation: DANIEL 010:003

King James: I ate no pleasant bread, neither came flesh nor wine in my mouth, neither did I anoint myself at all, till three whole weeks were fulfilled.

New International: I ate no choice food; no meat or wine touched my lips; and I used no lotions at all until the three weeks were over.

Blessing from God [161] Citation: HOSEA 002:008

King James: For she did not know that I gave her corn, and wine, and oil, and multiplied her silver and gold, which they prepared for Baal.

New International: She has not acknowledged that I was the one who gave her the grain, the new wine and oil, who lavished on her the silver and gold-- which they used for Baal.

Loss of wine is a curse from God [162] Citation: HOSEA 002:009

King James: Therefore will I return, and take away my corn in the time thereof, and my wine in the season thereof, and will recover my wool and my flax given to cover her nakedness.

New International: "Therefore I will take away my grain when it ripens, and my new wine when it is ready. I will take back my wool and my linen, intended to cover her nakedness.

Blessing from God [163] Citation: HOSEA 002:022

King James: And the earth shall hear the corn, and the wine, and the oil; and they shall hear Jezreel.

New International: and the earth will respond to the grain, the new wine and oil, and they will respond to Jezreel.

Abuse (examples of) [164] Citation: HOSEA 003:001

King James: Then said the Lord unto me, Go yet, love a woman beloved of her friend, yet an adulteress, according to the love of the Lord toward the children of Israel, who look to other gods, and love flagons of wine.

New International: The LORD said to me, "Go, show your love

to your wife again, though she is loved by another and is an adulteress. Love her as the LORD loves the Israelites, though they turn to other gods and love the sacred raisin cakes."

Abuse (examples of) [165] Citation: HOSEA 004:011

King James: Whoredom and wine and new wine take away the heart.

New International: to prostitution, to old wine and new, which take away the understanding

Abuse (examples of) [166] Citation: HOSEA 007:005

King James: In the day of our king the princes have made him sick with bottles of wine; he stretched out his hand with scorners.

New International: On the day of the festival of our king the princes become inflamed with wine, and he joins hands with the mockers.

Abuse (examples of) [167] Citation: HOSEA 007:014

King James: And they have not cried unto me with their heart, when they howled upon their beds: they assemble themselves for corn and wine, and they rebel against me.

New International: They do not cry out to me from their hearts but wail upon their beds. They gather together for grain and new wine but turn away from me.

Loss of wine is a curse from God [168] Citation: HOSEA 009:002

King James: The floor and the winepress shall not feed them, and the new wine shall fail in her.

New International: Threshing floors and winepresses will not feed the people; the new wine will fail them.

Offering (use in) [169] Citation: HOSEA 009:004

King James: They shall not offer wine offerings to the Lord, neither shall they be pleasing unto him: their sacrifices shall be unto them as the bread of mourners; all that eat thereof shall be polluted: for their bread for their soul shall not come into the house of the Lord.

New International: They will not pour out wine offerings to the LORD, nor will their sacrifices please him. Such sacrifices will be to them like the bread of mourners; all who eat them will be unclean. This food will be for themselves; it will not come into the temple of the LORD.

Blessing from God [170] Citation: HOSEA 014:007

King James: They that dwell under his shadow shall return; they shall revive as the corn, and grow as the vine: the scent thereof shall be as the wine of Lebanon.

New International: Men will dwell again in his shade. He will flourish like the grain. He will blossom like a vine, and his fame will be like the wine from Lebanon.

Loss of wine is a curse from God [171] Citation: JOEL 001:005

King James: Awake, ye drunkards, and weep; and howl, all ye drinkers of wine, because of the new wine; for it is cut off from your mouth.

New International: Wake up, you drunkards, and weep! Wail, all you drinkers of wine; wail because of the new wine, for it has been snatched from your lips.

Loss of wine is a curse from God [172] Citation: JOEL 001:010

King James: The field is wasted, the land mourneth; for the corn is wasted: the new wine is dried up, the oil languisheth.

New International: The fields are ruined, the ground is dried up ; the grain is destroyed, the new wine is dried up, the oil fails.

Blessing from God [173] Citation: JOEL 002:019

King James: Yea, the Lord will answer and say unto his people, Behold, I will send you corn, and wine, and oil, and ye shall be satisfied therewith: and I will no more make you a reproach among the heathen:

New International: The LORD will reply to them: `I am sending you grain, new wine and oil, enough to satisfy you fully; never again will I make you an object of scorn to the nations.

Blessing from God [174] Citation: JOEL 002:024

King James: And the floors shall be full of wheat, and the fats shall overflow with wine and oil.

New International: The threshing floors will be filled with grain; the vats will overflow with new wine and oil.

Abuse (examples of) [175] Citation: JOEL 003:003

King James: And they have cast lots for my people; and have given a boy for an harlot, and sold a girl for wine, that they might drink.

New International: They cast lots for my people and traded boys for prostitutes; they sold girls for wine that they might drink.

Blessing from God [176] Citation: JOEL 003:018

King James: And it shall come to pass in that day, that the mountains shall drop down new wine, and the hills shall flow with milk, and all the rivers of Judah shall flow with waters, and a fountain shall come forth of the house of the Lord, and shall water the valley of Shittim.

New International: `In that day the mountains will drip new wine, and the hills will flow with milk; all the ravines of Judah will run with water. A fountain will flow out of the LORD's house and will water the valley of acacias.

Vows of abstinence [177] Citation: AMOS 002:008

King James: And they lay themselves down upon clothes laid to pledge by every altar, and they drink the wine of the condemned in the house of their god.

New International: They lie down beside every altar on garments taken in pledge. In the house of their god they drink wine taken as fines.

Vows of abstinence [178] Citation: AMOS 002:012

King James: But ye gave the Nazarites wine to drink; and commanded the prophets, saying, Prophesy not.

New International: "But you made the Nazirites drink wine and commanded the prophets not to prophesy.

Loss of wine is a curse from God [179] Citation: AMOS 005:011

King James: Forasmuch therefore as your treading is upon the poor, and ye take from him burdens of wheat: ye have built houses of hewn stone, but ye shall not dwell in them; ye have planted pleasant vineyards, but ye shall not drink wine of them.

New International: You trample on the poor and force him to give you grain. Therefore, though you have built stone mansions, you will not live in them; though you have planted lush vineyards, you will not drink their wine.

Use is accepted as normal [180] Citation: AMOS 006:006

King James: That drink wine in bowls, and anoint themselves with the chief ointments: but they are not grieved for the affliction of Joseph.

New International: You drink wine by the bowlful and use the finest lotions, but you do not grieve over the ruin of Joseph.

Blessing from God [181] Citation: AMOS 009:013

King James: Behold, the days come, saith the Lord, that the plowman shall overtake the reaper, and the treader of grapes him that soweth seed; and the mountains shall drop sweet wine, and all the hills shall melt.

New International: "The days are coming," declares the LORD, "when the reaper will be overtaken by the plowman and the planter by the one treading grapes. New wine will drip from the mountains and flow from all the hills.

Blessing from God [182] Citation: AMOS 009:014

King James: And I will bring again the captivity of my people of Israel, and they shall build the waste cities, and inhabit them; and they shall plant vineyards, and drink the wine thereof; they shall also make gardens, and eat the fruit of them.

New International: I will bring back my exiled people Israel; they will rebuild the ruined cities and live in them. They will plant vineyards and drink their wine; they will make gardens and eat their fruit.

Abuse (examples of) [183] Citation: MICAH 002:011

King James: If a man walking in the spirit and falsehood do lie, saying, I will prophesy unto thee of wine and of strong drink; he shall even be the prophet of this people.

New International: If a liar and deceiver comes and says, `I will prophesy for you plenty of wine and beer,' he would be just the prophet for this people!

Loss of wine is a curse from God [184] Citation: MICAH 006:015

King James: Thou shalt sow, but thou shalt not reap; thou shalt tread the olives, but thou shalt not anoint thee with oil; and sweet wine, but shalt not drink wine.

New International: You will plant but not harvest; you will press olives but not use the oil on yourselves, you will crush grapes but not drink the wine.

Symbolic [185] Citation: NAHUM 001:010

King James: For while they be folden together as thorns, and while they are drunken as drunkards, they shall be devoured as stubble fully dry.

New International: They will be entangled among thorns and drunk from their wine; they will be consumed like dry stubble.

Abuse (examples of) [186] Citation: HABAKKUK 002:005

King James: Yea also, because he transgresseth by wine, he is a proud man, neither keepeth at home, who enlargeth his desire as hell, and is as death, and cannot be satisfied, but gathereth unto him all nations, and heapeth unto him all people:

New International: indeed, wine betrays him; he is arrogant and never at rest. Because he is as greedy as the grave and like death is never satisfied, he gathers to himself all the nations and takes captive all the peoples.

Symbolic [187] Citation: ZEPHANIAH 001:012

King James: And it shall come to pass at that time, that I will search Jerusalem with candles, and punish the men that are settled on their lees: that say in their heart, The Lord will not do good, neither will he do evil.

New International: At that time I will search Jerusalem with lamps and punish those who are complacent, who are like wine left on its dregs, who think, `The LORD will do nothing, either good or bad.'

Loss of wine is a curse from God [188] Citation: ZEPHANIAH 001:013

King James: Therefore their goods shall become a booty, and their houses a desolation: they shall also build houses, but not inhabit them; and they shall plant vineyards, but not drink the wine thereof.

New International: Their wealth will be plundered, their houses demolished. They will build houses but not live in them; they will plant vineyards but not drink the wine.

Loss of wine is a curse from God [189] Citation: HAGGAI 001:011

King James: And I called for a drought upon the land, and upon the mountains, and upon the corn, and upon the new wine, and upon the oil, and upon that which the ground bringeth forth, and upon men, and upon cattle, and upon all the labour of the hands.

New International: I called for a drought on the fields and the mountains, on the grain, the new wine, the oil and whatever the ground produces, on men and cattle, and on the labor of your hands."

Use is accepted as normal [190] Citation: HAGGAI 002:012

King James: If one bear holy flesh in the skirt of his garment, and with his skirt do touch bread, or pottage, or wine, or oil, or any meat, shall it be holy? And the priests answered and said, No.

New International: If a person carries consecrated meat in the fold of his garment, and that fold touches some bread or stew, some wine, oil or other food, does it become consecrated?"' The priests answered,

"No."

Use is accepted as normal [191] Citation: HAGGAI 002:016

King James: Since those days were, when one came to an heap of twenty measures, there were but ten: when one came to the pressfat for to draw out fifty vessels out of the press, there were but twenty.

New International: When anyone came to a heap of twenty measures, there were only ten. When anyone went to a wine vat to draw fifty measures, there were only twenty.

Symbolic [192] Citation: ZECHARIAH 009:015

King James: The Lord of hosts shall defend them; and they shall devour, and subdue with sling stones; and they shall drink, and make a noise as through wine; and they shall be filled like bowls, and as the corners of the altar.

New International: and the LORD Almighty will shield them. They will destroy and overcome with slingstones. They will drink and roar as with wine; they will be full like a bowl used for sprinkling the corners of the altar.

Blessing from God [193] Citation: ZECHARIAH 009:017

King James: For how great is his goodness, and how great is his beauty! corn shall make the young men cheerful, and new wine the maids.

New International: How attractive and beautiful they will be! Grain will make the young men thrive, and new wine the young women.

Symbolic [194] Citation: ZECHARIAH 010:007

King James: And they of Ephraim shall be like a mighty man, and their heart shall rejoice as through wine: yea, their children shall see it, and be glad; their heart shall rejoice in the Lord.

New International: The Ephraimites will become like mighty men, and their hearts will be glad as with wine. Their children will see it and be joyful; their hearts will rejoice in the LORD.

Symbolic [195] Citation: MATTHEW 009:017

King James: Neither do men put new wine into old bottles: else the bottles break, and the wine runneth out, and the bottles perish: but they put new wine into new bottles, and both are preserved.

New International: Neither do men pour new wine into old wineskins. If they do, the skins will burst, the wine will run out and the wineskins will be ruined. No, they pour new wine into new wineskins, and both are preserved."

Use is accepted as normal [196] Citation: MATTHEW 027:034

King James: They gave him vinegar to drink mingled with gall: and when he had tasted thereof, he would not drink.

New International: There they offered Jesus wine to drink, mixed with gall; but after tasting it, he refused to drink it.

Use is accepted as normal [197] Citation: MATTHEW 027:048

King James: And straightway one of them ran, and took a spunge, and filled it with vinegar, and put it on a reed, and gave him to drink.

New International: Immediately one of them ran and got a sponge. He filled it with wine vinegar, put it on a stick, and offered it to Jesus to drink.

Symbolic [198] Citation: MARK 002:022

King James: And no man putteth new wine into old bottles: else the new wine doth burst the bottles, and the wine is spilled, and the bottles will be marred: but new wine must be put into new bottles.

New International: And no one pours new wine into old wineskins. If he does, the wine will burst the skins, and both the wine and the wineskins will be ruined. No, he pours new wine into new wineskins."

Use is accepted as normal [199] Citation: MARK 015:023

King James: And they gave him to drink wine mingled with myrrh: but he received it not.

New International: Then they offered him wine mixed with myrrh, but he did not take it.

Use is accepted as normal [200] Citation: MARK 015:036

King James: And one ran and filled a spunge full of vinegar, and put it on a reed, and gave him to drink, saying, Let alone; let us see whether Elias will come to take him down.

New International: One man ran, filled a sponge with wine vinegar, put it on a stick, and offered it to Jesus to drink. "Now leave him alone. Let's see if Elijah comes to take him down," he said.

Vows of abstinence [201] Citation: LUKE 001:015

King James: For he shall be great in the sight of the Lord, and shall drink neither wine nor strong drink; and he shall be filled with the Holy Ghost, even from his mother's womb.

New International: for he will be great in the sight of the Lord. He is never to take wine or other fermented drink, and he will be filled with the Holy Spirit even from birth.

Symbolic [202] Citation: LUKE 005:037

King James: And no man putteth new wine into old bottles; else the new wine will burst the bottles, and be spilled, and the bottles shall perish.

New International: And no one pours new wine into old wineskins. If he does, the new wine will burst the skins, the wine will run out and the wineskins will be ruined.

Symbolic [203] Citation: LUKE 005:038

King James: But new wine must be put into new bottles; and both are preserved.

New International: No, new wine must be poured into new wineskins.

Symbolic [204] Citation: LUKE 005:039

King James: No man also having drunk old wine straightway desireth new: for he saith, the old is better.

New International: And no one after drinking old wine wants the new, for he says, `The old is better.'"

Vows of abstinence [205] Citation: LUKE 007:033

King James: For John the Baptist came neither eating bread nor drinking wine; and ye say, He hath a devil.

New International: For John the Baptist came neither eating bread nor drinking wine, and you say, `He has a demon.'

Use is accepted as normal [206] Citation: LUKE 010:034

King James: And went to him, and bound up his wounds, pouring in oil and wine, and set him on his own beast, and brought him to an inn, and took care of him.

New International: He went to him and bandaged his wounds, pouring on oil and wine. Then he put the man on his own donkey, took him to an inn and took care of him.

Use is accepted as normal [207] Citation: LUKE 023:036

King James: And the soldiers also mocked him, coming to him, and offering him vinegar,

New International: The soldiers also came up and mocked him. They offered him wine vinegar

Use is accepted as normal [208] Citation: JOHN 002:003

King James: And when they wanted wine, the mother of Jesus saith unto him, They have no wine.

New International: When the wine was gone, Jesus' mother said to him, "They have no more wine."

Use is accepted as normal [209] Citation: JOHN 002:009

King James: When the ruler of the feast had tasted the water that was made wine, and knew not whence it was: (but the servants which drew the water knew;) the governor of the feast called the bridegroom,

New International: and the master of the banquet tasted the water that had been turned into wine. He did not realize where it had come from, though the servants who had drawn the water knew. Then he called the bridegroom aside

Use is accepted as normal [210] Citation: JOHN 002:010

King James: And saith unto him, Every man at the beginning doth set forth good wine; and when men have well drunk, then that which is worse: but thou hast kept the good wine until now.

New International: and said, "Everyone brings out the choice wine first and then the cheaper wine after the guests have had too much to drink; but you have saved the best till now."

Use is accepted as normal [211] Citation: JOHN 004:046

King James: So Jesus came again into Cana of Galilee, where he made the water wine. And there was a certain nobleman, whose son was sick at Capernaum.

New International: Once more he visited Cana in Galilee, where he had turned the water into wine. And there was a certain royal official whose son lay sick at Capernaum.

Use is accepted as normal [212] Citation: JOHN 019:029

King James: Now there was set a vessel full of vinegar: and they filled a spunge with vinegar, and put it upon hyssop, and put it to his mouth.

New International: A jar of wine vinegar was there, so they soaked a sponge in it, put the sponge on a stalk of the hyssop plant, and lifted it to Jesus' lips.

False accusations of drunkeness [213] Citation: ACTS 002:013

King James: Others mocking said, These men are full of new wine.

New International: Some, however, made fun of them and said, "They have had too much wine. "

Exception (the only verse like this) [214] Citation: ROMANS 014:021

King James: It is good neither to eat flesh, nor to drink wine, nor any thing whereby thy brother stumbleth, or is offended, or is made weak.

New International: It is better not to eat meat or drink wine or to do anything else that will cause your brother to fall.

Warnings against abuse [215] Citation: EPHESIANS 005:018

King James: And be not drunk with wine, wherein is excess; but be filled with the Spirit;

New International: Do not get drunk on wine, which leads to debauchery. Instead, be filled with the Spirit.

Deacons (rules for) [216] Citation: 1 TIMOTHY 003:003

King James: Not given to wine, no striker, not greedy of filthy lucre; but patient, not a brawler, not covetous;

New International: not given to drunkenness, not violent but gentle, not quarrelsome, not a lover of money.

Deacons (rules for) [217] Citation: 1 TIMOTHY 003:008

King James: Likewise must the deacons be grave, not doubletongued, not given to much wine, not greedy of filthy lucre;

New International: Deacons, likewise, are to be men worthy of respect, sincere, not indulging in much wine, and not pursuing dishonest gain.

Use is accepted as normal [218] Citation: 1 TIMOTHY 005:023

King James: Drink no longer water, but use a little wine for thy stomach's sake and thine often infirmities.

New International: Stop drinking only water, and use a little wine because of your stomach and your frequent illnesses.

Deacons (rules for) [219] Citation: TITUS 001:007

King James: For a bishop must be blameless, as the steward of God; not selfwilled, not soon angry, not given to wine, no striker, not given to filthy lucre;

New International: Since an overseer is entrusted with God's work, he must be blameless--not overbearing, not quick-tempered, not given to drunkenness, not violent, not pursuing dishonest gain.

Warnings against abuse [220] Citation: TITUS 002:003

King James: The aged women likewise, that they be in behaviour as

becometh holiness, not false accusers, not given to much wine, teachers
of good things;

New International: Likewise, teach the older women to be reverent
in the way they live, not to be slanderers or addicted to much wine, but
to teach what is good.

Warnings against abuse [221] Citation: 1 PETER 004:003

King James: For the time past of our life may suffice us to have
wrought the will of the Gentiles, when we walked in lasciviousness,
lusts, excess of wine, revellings, banquetings, and abominable idolatries:

New International: For you have spent enough time in the past
doing what pagans choose to do--living in debauchery, lust, drunkenness,
orgies, carousing and detestable idolatry.

Symbolic [222] Citation: REVELATION 006:006

King James: And I heard a voice in the midst of the four beasts
say, A measure of wheat for a penny, and three measures of barley for a
penny; and see thou hurt not the oil and the wine.

New International: Then I heard what sounded like a voice among
the four living creatures, saying, "A quart of wheat for a day's wages,
and three quarts of barley for a day's wages, and do not damage the oil
and the wine!"

Symbolic [223] Citation: REVELATION 014:008

King James: And there followed another angel, saying, Babylon is
fallen, is fallen, that great city, because she made all nations drink of the
wine of the wrath of her fornication.

New International: A second angel followed and said, "Fallen!
Fallen is Babylon the Great, which made all the nations drink the
maddening wine of her adulteries."

Symbolic [224] Citation: REVELATION 014:010

King James: The same shall drink of the wine of the wrath of God,
which is poured out without mixture into the cup of his indignation; and
he shall be tormented with fire and brimstone in the presence of the holy

angels, and in the presence of the Lamb:

New International: he, too, will drink of the wine of God's fury, which has been poured full strength into the cup of his wrath. He will be tormented with burning sulfur in the presence of the holy angels and of the Lamb.

Symbolic [225] Citation: REVELATION 016:019

King James: And the great city was divided into three parts, and the cities of the nations fell: and great Babylon came in remembrance before God, to give unto her the cup of the wine of the fierceness of his wrath.

New International: The great city split into three parts, and the cities of the nations collapsed. God remembered Babylon the Great and gave her the cup filled with the wine of the fury of his wrath.

Symbolic [226] Citation: REVELATION 017:002

King James: With whom the kings of the earth have committed fornication, and the inhabitants of the earth have been made drunk with the wine of her fornication.

New International: With her the kings of the earth committed adultery and the inhabitants of the earth were intoxicated with the wine of her adulteries."

Symbolic [227] Citation: REVELATION 018:003

King James: For all nations have drunk of the wine of the wrath of her fornication, and the kings of the earth have committed fornication with her, and the merchants of the earth are waxed rich through the abundance of her delicacies.

New International: For all the nations have drunk the maddening wine of her adulteries. The kings of the earth committed adultery with her, and the merchants of the earth grew rich from her excessive luxuries."

Symbolic [228] Citation: REVELATION 018:013

King James: And cinnamon, and odours, and ointments, and frankincense, and wine, and oil, and fine flour, and wheat, and beasts, and sheep, and horses, and chariots, and slaves, and souls of men.

New International: cargoes of cinnamon and spice, of incense, myrrh and frankincense, of wine and olive oil, of fine flour and wheat; cattle and sheep; horses and carriages; and bodies and souls of men.

References to STRONG DRINK (19)

Vows of abstinence [1] Citation: LEVITICUS 010:009

King James: Do not drink wine nor strong drink, thou, nor thy sons with thee, when ye go into the tabernacle of the congregation, lest ye die: it shall be a statute for ever throughout your generations:

New International: "You and your sons are not to drink wine or other fermented drink whenever you go into the Tent of Meeting, or you will die. This is a lasting ordinance for the generations to come.

Vows of abstinence [2] Citation: NUMBERS 006:003

King James: He shall separate himself from wine and strong drink, and shall drink no vinegar of wine, or vinegar of strong drink, neither shall he drink any liquor of grapes, nor eat moist grapes, or dried.

New International: he must abstain from wine and other fermented drink and must not drink vinegar made from wine or from other fermented drink. He must not drink grape juice or eat grapes or raisins.

Offering (use in) [3] Citation: DEUTERONOMY 014:026

King James: And thou shalt bestow that money for whatsoever thy soul lusteth after, for oxen, or for sheep, or for wine, or for strong drink, or for whatsoever thy soul desireth: and thou shalt eat there before the Lord thy God, and thou shalt rejoice, thou, and thine household,

New International: Use the silver to buy whatever you like: cattle, sheep, wine or other fermented drink, or anything you wish. Then you and your household shall eat there in the presence of the LORD your God and rejoice.

No specific category [4] Citation: DEUTERONOMY 029:006

King James: Ye have not eaten bread, neither have ye drunk wine or strong drink: that ye might know that I am the Lord your God.

New International: You ate no bread and drank no wine or other fermented drink. I did this so that you might know that I am the LORD your God.

Vows of abstinence [5] Citation: JUDGES 013:004

King James: Now therefore beware, I pray thee, and drink not wine nor strong drink, and eat not any unclean thing:

New International: Now see to it that you drink no wine or other fermented drink and that you do not eat anything unclean,

Vows of abstinence [6] Citation: JUDGES 013:007

King James: But he said unto me, Behold, thou shalt conceive, and bear a son; and now drink no wine nor strong drink, neither eat any unclean thing: for the child shall be a Nazarite to God from the womb to the day of his death.

New International: But he said to me, `You will conceive and give birth to a son. Now then, drink no wine or other fermented drink and do not eat anything unclean, because the boy will be a Nazarite of God from birth until the day of his death.'"

Vows of abstinence [7] Citation: JUDGES 013:014

King James: She may not eat of any thing that cometh of the vine, neither let her drink wine or strong drink, nor eat any unclean thing: all that I commanded her let her observe.

New International: She must not eat anything that comes from the grapevine, nor drink any wine or other fermented drink nor eat anything unclean. She must do everything I have commanded her."

False accusations of drunkeness [8] Citation: 1 SAMUEL 001:015

King James: And Hannah answered and said, No, my lord, I am a woman of a sorrowful spirit: I have drunk neither wine nor strong drink, but have poured out my soul before the Lord.

New International: "Not so, my lord," Hannah replied, "I am a woman who is deeply troubled. I have not been drinking wine or beer; I was pouring out my soul to the LORD.

Warnings against abuse [9] Citation: PROVERBS 020:001

King James: Wine is a mocker, strong drink is raging: and whosoever is deceived thereby is not wise.

New International: Wine is a mocker and beer a brawler; whoever is led astray by them is not wise.

Warnings against abuse [10] Citation: PROVERBS 031:004

King James: It is not for kings, O Lemuel, it is not for kings to drink wine; nor for princes strong drink:

New International: "It is not for kings, O Lemuel-- not for kings to drink wine, not for rulers to crave beer,

Use is accepted as normal [11] Citation: PROVERBS 031:006

King James: Give strong drink unto him that is ready to perish, and wine unto those that be of heavy hearts.

New International: Give beer to those who are perishing, wine to those who are in anguish;

Warnings against abuse [12] Citation: ISAIAH 005:011

King James: Woe unto them that rise up early in the morning, that they may follow strong drink; that continue until night, till wine inflame them!

New International: Woe to those who rise early in the morning to run after their drinks, who stay up late at night till they are inflamed with wine.

Warnings against abuse [13] Citation: ISAIAH 005:022

King James: Woe unto them that are mighty to drink wine, and men of strength to mingle strong drink:

New International: Woe to those who are heroes at drinking wine and champions at mixing drinks,

Loss of wine is a curse from God [14] Citation: ISAIAH 024:009

King James: They shall not drink wine with a song; strong drink shall be bitter to them that drink it.

New International: No longer do they drink wine with a song; the beer is bitter to its drinkers.

Abuse (examples of) [15] Citation: ISAIAH 028:007

King James: But they also have erred through wine, and through strong drink are out of the way; the priest and the prophet have erred through strong drink, they are swallowed up of wine, they are out of the way through strong drink; they err in vision, they stumble in judgment.

New International: And these also stagger from wine and reel from beer: Priests and prophets stagger from beer and are befuddled with wine; they reel from beer, they stagger when seeing visions, they stumble when rendering decisions.

Symbolic [16] Citation: ISAIAH 029:009

King James: Stay yourselves, and wonder; cry ye out, and cry: they are drunken, but not with wine; they stagger, but not with strong drink.

New International: Be stunned and amazed, blind yourselves and be sightless; be drunk, but not from wine, stagger, but not from beer.

Abuse (examples of) [17] Citation: ISAIAH 056:012

King James: Come ye, say they, I will fetch wine, and we will fill ourselves with strong drink; and to morrow shall be as this day, and much more abundant.

New International: "Come," each one cries, "let me get wine! Let us drink our fill of beer! And tomorrow will be like today, or even far better."

Abuse (examples of) [18] Citation: MICAH 002:011

King James: If a man walking in the spirit and falsehood do lie, saying, I will prophesy unto thee of wine and of strong drink; he shall even be the prophet of this people.

New International: If a liar and deceiver comes and says, `I will prophesy for you plenty of wine and beer,' he would be just the prophet for this people!

Vows of abstinence [19] Citation: LUKE 001:015

King James: For he shall be great in the sight of the Lord, and shall drink neither wine nor strong drink; and he shall be filled with the Holy Ghost, even from his mother's womb.

New International: for he will be great in the sight of the Lord. He is never to take wine or other fermented drink, and he will be filled with the Holy Spirit even from birth.

Made in the USA
San Bernardino, CA
05 July 2016